COPING W...

ANITA NAIK was born in London. She worked ...
Seventeen for four years before becoming a freelance journalist. She now writes the advice column for *Just Seventeen* and *The Evening Times* in Scotland and freelance articles for a variety of publications, including *New Woman, 19, Smash Hits* and *More*. This is her third book.

Overcoming Common Problems

COPING WITH CRUSHES

Anita Naik

sheldon PRESS

First published in Great Britain in 1994 by
Sheldon Press, SPCK, Marylebone Road, London NW1 4DU

© Anita Naik 1994

All rights reserved. No part of this book may be reproduced or transmitted in
any form or by any means, electronic or mechanical, including photocopying,
recording, or by any information storage and retrieval system, without
permission in writing from the publisher.

Extract on page vii from 'I'm not in love' (words and music by Graham
Gouldman and Eric Stewart), © 1975, reproduced by permission of EMI
Music Publishing Ltd, London WC2H OEA

British Library Cataloguing-in-Publication Data
A catalogue record for this book is available from the British Library

ISBN 0–85969–700–2

Photoset by Deltatype Ltd, Ellesmere Port, Cheshire
Printed in Great Britain by Biddles Ltd, Guildford and King's Lynn

Contents

	Acknowledgements	vi
	Introduction	vii
1	What are Crushes and Why Do We Get Them?	1
2	The Positive Side of Crushes	13
3	The Negative Side of Crushes	22
4	Crushes on Famous People	34
5	Crushes on Older Men	48
6	Crushes on Girls	56
7	Crushes That Come True	65
8	When a Crush Becomes an Obsession	74
9	Boys With Crushes	83
10	Crushes on Boys	93
	Useful Addresses	102

Acknowledgements

With grateful thanks to Leesa Daniels for her expertise and encouragement. And special thanks to all the *Just 17* readers and people who so readily supplied the case histories for this book.

Introduction

> I'm not in love,
> So don't forget it.
> It's just a silly phase I'm going through.
> *10 CC* 'I'm Not In Love'

When I was fourteen years old I developed a crush on a pop star. I spent the whole of the next year collecting every single piece of information I could find on him. I stuck pictures of him all over my bedroom walls, played his records over and over, and watched every TV show he was on, until my brothers threatened to tear up all my posters. I even got tickets to his concert and though I was seated amidst two thousand screaming girls I was convinced he sang each song especially for me. My mother still tells a very embarrassing story that has me running madly down a road following his speeding car, screaming out his name.

Nearly thirteen years later, I can still remember every little detail about that crush. I can tell you what his date of birth is, what kind of food he ate, where he shopped and even the kind of underpants he wore. I can also tell you how exhilarating and exciting it was to be in the midst of a crush. At the same time I can also tell of how demoralizing it was to have no one (apart from one friend) who understood just how deep my feelings went. Whenever I tried to explain it to anyone else they'd retort 'Oh, it's only a crush, you'll grow out of it'. The trouble was, I didn't want to grow out of it, and I didn't believe I ever would.

In the six years I've worked on *Just 17*'s advice pages, and the two as the advice columnist, I've realized that when it comes to crushes, nothing has changed. Each week hundreds of girls write to me, desperately unhappy or confused because they have fallen madly in love with their teachers/friends/actors/pop stars. They suffer the same hope and frustration that 'real' love brings, and

INTRODUCTION

yet they receive none of the sympathy and understanding a run-of-the-mill relationship gets. Nearly all of these girls are left to feel guilty, misunderstood, and somewhat foolish for their feelings.

Unrequited love is painful but it can also be memorable and teach you a few things about the nature of love. This book is designed to help you understand and learn how to deal with crushes without feeling you're going completely mad. It also offers some insight through other people's experiences and shows how crushes can be both a good and an undaunting experience.

Just as a small postscript, I'd like to add that when I was 23 years old I actually got to interview the pop star I had had my first teenage crush on. The day before I went to meet him, I remembered all the feelings, fantasies and emotions I used to have about him and couldn't believe I now felt so sane about him. In the flesh he was nice but quite unlike the person I imagined him to be. In fact, the boys I've been out with in the intervening years have been closer to the mark than he actually was. He did tell me one interesting thing though: he admitted to having a crush on a singer when he was 15 years old. A crush that actually led him to becoming a pop star!

1
What are Crushes and Why Do We Get Them?

Ask anyone to tell you about the first person they ever fell in love with and you're likely to find out it was someone they had never ever spoken to or really known. The fact is, we've all had a crush at some point in our lives, and no matter how much time passes, most of us can still remember them. The Oxford Dictionary describes a crush as an infatuation, yet, for anyone who has ever had a crush or is at present in the midst of one, you'll know this definition is a huge understatement. Below, a group of girls aged between 13 and 18 define just what a crush means to them:

'A crush is just the same as being in love.' *Donna (17)*
'Unrequited love.' *Josie (15)*
'Being in love with someone you don't know.' *Laura (15)*
'A miserable way of being in love.' *Kim (14)*
'Exciting.' *Helen (16)*
'A secret love.' *Sue (17)*
'A waste of time.' *Gail (16)*
'Good fun if you keep them in perspective.' *Lisa (18)*
'Being in love without all the bad parts.' *Alice (17)*
'A first step into love.' *Jacqui (15)*
'A bizarre emotion that hits you and knocks your life out of control.' *Jenny (17)*

As you can see, for most people a crush is an intangible, baffling force of nature. A force that makes you fall in love with someone you don't really know. For some people a crush is an ideal relationship; for others it becomes a nightmare. A crush is basically a relationship that goes on between you and what you fantasize a person to be like. Whether you agree with this or not,

WHAT ARE CRUSHES AND WHY DO WE GET THEM?

one thing is for sure, crushes are undoubtedly powerful, intensive and overwhelming. Despite what some people may say, I doubt very much that there is one person alive who has not had a crush on someone at one point in their life. It may have lasted two days, two weeks or two years, but the depth of emotions felt are likely to have been the same: exhilaration, despair, unfathomable happiness and incredible sadness.

> The first time I had a crush I didn't know what had hit me. One day I was quite happy the next I was madly in love with a guy I didn't even know. It seemed he was on my mind 100 times a day. I couldn't do anything without imagining what he'd do in the same situation. In the two months I had a crush on him I don't think there was one emotion I didn't go through. I was either blissfully happy, sad, tearful, depressed and/or excited all because of him. It was all very confusing.
> *Helen (15)*

Living with a crush is comparable to going on a roller-coaster ride. It's exciting, frightening, and scary. At times you want to get off, but for the most part you're glad you went through with it. For some people, the ride is so exciting that they get on it time and time again, while for others once is more than enough.

> I'm not embarrassed to admit I've had a crush but I hope I never go through it again. It was awful because no one was at all sympathetic and there were times I felt like I was going mad. I mean it's crazy to think you're in love with someone you hardly know.
> *Julie (16)*

> Sometimes being in love with someone I don't know is hard. It makes me depressed and sad because I feel I'm wasting my time on someone who isn't real. My friends all say, why bother if it makes me unhappy but the high points make it worthwhile.
> *Jacqui (15)*

WHAT ARE CRUSHES AND WHY DO WE GET THEM?

The trouble with crushes is people love to ridicule them. They think just because the relationship isn't real to them, then the feelings and emotions the person with a crush is feeling aren't real either. The common notion being, if a crush is that hard to deal with why do people bother with them. The answer is simple, a crush isn't that easy to control. You can't just turn it off and on like a tap. If you're in the midst of one and it's making you unhappy it's nearly impossible to walk away from it.

> I know what some people think of me because they can't wait to tell me. My friends think I am a pathetic person who can't face 'real life' and 'real boys' all because I choose to have a crush on an actor, rather than someone in my class.
> *Lisa (14)*

> When I was 14 years old, I got a crush on my teacher, everyone was so unsympathetic. They thought I would grow out of it and would just laugh at me. Whenever I was sad over him, and felt depressed my parents would just laugh and say I didn't know what I was talking about. That really hurt because I felt they were be-littling my feelings. I felt if these feelings made me cry and be depressed, who was to say that they weren't real. To me they were all very real.
> *Anna (18)*

If you have ever had a crush you'll know the truth of Anna's comment. What's more, you'll know just how isolating and upsetting a crush can be because the emotional impact is just the same as a 'real' relationship. At the same time you'll also recognize how a crush has the power to make you fleetingly contented at the same time as making you desperately unhappy.

> I go through about a thousand feelings all at the same time when I see him on TV. I feel happy that he's so close, but also feel so depressed because I'm not part of his life.
> *Kim (14)*

WHAT ARE CRUSHES AND WHY DO WE GET THEM?

I spent a whole month getting excited about seeing him in concert. I went shopping especially for the right clothes, had my hair done and talked endlessly about it for weeks. I really felt like I was going on a date with him, even though I knew there'd be over 20,000 other girls there. The trouble was once I got there, and really saw how many girls liked him as much as me, my happiness turned into misery and I cried my way through the whole concert.
Laura (15)

Crushes don't just afflict young people. If more people were honest about their emotions, we'd see that not only are crushes extremely common but that they can affect anyone at any age. They materialize for a variety of reasons: they can be a first step into love, or a way to get over heartbreak, they can even be a way to escape the mundaneness of life. The truth is, most of us do succumb to crushes, without ever knowing what's hit us and why.

Why do we all fall in love?

In order to look at crushes we have first to see just why it is we fall in love. According to scientists, love is a chemical reaction. Anthony Walsh, author of *The Science of Love: Understanding Love and Its Effects on Mind and Body*, says: 'Phenylethylamine (PEA) is the chemical responsible. It gives you that silly smile that you flash at strangers. When we meet someone who is attractive to us, the whistle blows at the PEA factory.'

Lovers often claim that they feel like they are being swept away. This is because they are being flooded with chemicals, thanks to a meeting of eyes, a touch, or a particular smell.

I just have to spot him on the street and I feel a warm flush go through my body. It's like I've just taken a happy pill or something. It's such a wonderful feeling, no wonder I won't

make myself stop thinking about him. Why should I give up this brilliant feeling.
Donna (16)

PEA is the chemical responsible for this warm feeling. It's the cause of the reaction that occurs when you find yourself madly attracted to someone. Of course, the initial attraction is based purely on looks; after all, you don't know them enough to base it on anything else. And basically you have to be attracted to the way another person looks before their presence will even register in your mind. This doesn't mean they have to be the most beautiful thing that ever walked the earth. There are always other factors at work, which is why you may think someone you fall in love with is stunningly attractive, while your friends can't stand the sight of him.

After all, the PEA rush can fool your emotions completely, especially if it's the first time you've ever experienced such a rush.

> The first time our new teacher walked into the classroom I felt my mouth dry up, my knees shake and my heart pound, and it was such a shocking feeling. My thinking was, I must feel like this for a reason and that reason must be love. Now I can see it was just sexual attraction but because I had never experienced anything like this before I was sure it meant more.
> *Clare (18)*

It's important to take these mixed emotions, chemical rushes, and acute feelings of love as they come and not to try and over-analyse them to the extent that you see them as some sort of 'sign' that you're both meant to be together.

> I went from being a normal 13 year old, to this mad thing that was madly and passionately in love with a pop star. Every time I saw him on TV I'd cry my eyes out, then I'd watch his video over and over. I'd also rush to the shops every week and buy

up all the magazines with him in and talk about him constantly. I was convinced we were meant to be together because I'd never behaved like this before. Now I can see it was just the first time I'd been attracted to someone and I blew it all out of proportion.
Lena (17)

Remember, we are all attracted to different features in other people, which is why there is really someone for everyone. Biologically we're a mating species, and in order to reproduce we can't all fall for the same people. With crushes, even if we fall for the same person as someone else, we're likely to be attracted to different things.

Karen and I both fell for the same pop star but it was weird. I liked him because he was funny and loud. But she liked him because he was into the environment and seemed to really care about everything.
Becky (16)

Psychologically, we're likely to fall for someone who resembles us. Jonathan Gathorne Hardy says in his book, *Love, Sex, Marriage And Divorce*, 'On the whole, people tend to fall in love with someone of the same level of attractiveness as themselves.' This is because it promotes feelings of security and comfort.

Scientists also believe that each person carries in his or her mind a unique unconscious guide to their ideal partner, a so-called 'love map'. Drawn from our childhood, the map is a record of whatever we found enticing, exciting or disgusting through our lives. This could be anything from a person who made us laugh to an incident that made us cry. Early relationships are very important here, because often people we learn to trust and like early in our lives help create a pattern for all our later relationships and friendships. All this information is gathered while we are growing up and imprinted in our brains by the time we reach adolescence.

Our 'love maps' are completely unique and different. Some people find that they like being cuddled, others prefer space; all this comes from early childhood and the way we received love from our parents. Of course, your requirements may be a blond, tall doctor who tells jokes and likes holding your hand, but you may not actually end up with that. Partners never meet each and every requirement, but meeting someone who is tall and tells jokes may strike up enough wires to indicate love to your brain and cause a PEA rush. Even if the people you are attracted to all look different, there may be a non-physical factor that draws you to them. For instance, Liz is 20 years old and grew up with just her mum in a very small village in Wales. She has had crushes since she was 11 years old. None of her crushes resemble each other but they are all on older famous men with glamorous lifestyles. She has never been out with anyone because she says this is the only type of person she is looking for and no one else will do.

> Despite what my friends say to me, they don't date lots of different types of men. If you take a look at their boyfriends, each of them always go for the same type and always have done. This is the same with me but my problem is most of the men I like are out of my reach. So I often have to get my fill of them by going to the cinema or watching a video. Okay, so I don't have them with me, but the feelings I have for them are the same ones my friends have for their boyfriends.
> *Liz (20)*

Do we pick our crushes?

The fact is, crushes aren't always chosen. Often we won't have even noticed someone and then suddenly, without any great revelation, they become the best thing in the world. This has more to do with ourselves than the person we have chosen. Crushes arrive at opportune moments in our life: when we're ready to learn about love, when we're getting over a failed love affair, when we're bored with the mundaneness of life, and when we need a driving force to get us moving. This is why crushes come and go throughout our lives and why they should never be dismissed as a silly phase or a fake love affair.

> Mr Carter was the first teacher I ever had who helped me to believe in myself. Everyone else had me down as a trouble maker with no brains. He encouraged me to work and I ended up passing all my exams because I wanted him to be proud of me. You see, by then I was madly in love with him. I confessed it to him once and he was very nice but told me firmly that he was married. Now it seems so silly. You see he was fifty years old with a bald head – hardly a heart throb. But he was also the first man in my life to ever believe in me and tell me I was good at something.
> *Christine (23)*

Its the very vulnerability of life around adolescence that makes crushes hit home harder. Most of us feel our bodies aren't right, no one understands us, and somehow we're still caught between wanting to be an adult and desperately clinging to our childhood. A crush can often be our only solace at this time.

> My feelings for this famous actor were the only things that kept me going when I was 14 years old. He understood me, liked me for what I was, thought I was attractive and never hassled me. It's no wonder I fell in love with him.
> *Anna (19)*

Adolescence makes everything look worse and scary because it's a time of transformation and change. Our body starts to mature and our hormones are activated. Suddenly those spotty boys we

WHAT ARE CRUSHES AND WHY DO WE GET THEM?

used to ridicule become attractive and appealing. Then there is the pressure from everyone to be part of a couple and fall in love. Everything you look at seems to say that in order to be a successful person you need to have someone in love with you. Obviously, if you don't, then there must be something wrong with you.

> I'm dying to be in love because it looks so great. Everyone says it's something that makes your whole life better and more exciting and I agree. What could be better than waking up and thinking of someone you're in love with and that feeling being with you all day.
> *Sue (15)*

As Sue points out, we're all eager to taste love, to see what it feels like and how it affects us. It's this longing that is highly addictive and that leads us to look for someone with the ideals we want. Donna is such a girl. Since she was 12 years old she has fallen in and out of crushes.

> I like being in love or should I say I like having a crush. In fact, I'm aware that I talk myself into crushes. I'll be watching a film and a good looking man will come on. I'll then think, 'He's nice, I wonder what he'd be like to go out with.' If his character's nice then I'll imagine dating him. I'll build up all kinds of fantasies about him. Then before I know it I'll have a crush on him and think I'm in love. Sometimes, these crushes only last a couple of weeks but my longest one lasted nearly a year.
> *Donna (16)*

Apart from the media pressure to fall in love there is also the pressure that comes from our nearest and dearest. Parents are always asking their kids if they've got a boyfriend or girlfriend yet. Their good-natured teasing may be funny to them but many don't realize the pressure they put their kids under.

WHAT ARE CRUSHES AND WHY DO WE GET THEM?

I feel like such a failure in my mother's eyes. She desperately wants me to have a boyfriend and fall in love. When I had a crush on this boy down the road she was really interested and would get me to talk about him all the time. I never went out with him but I kept pretending it was about to happen because I liked the fact I was suddenly interesting to my mother.
Kelly (14)

The same kind of pressure comes from friends. Different people fall in love at different times but it's hard to see this when all your friends seem to be falling in love and you're not. You may think 'What's wrong with me?' 'What have they got, that I haven't?' and 'Is it normal not to be in love?' The answer is, there is no set age to fall in love. No written law that says 'If you haven't got a boyfriend by the time you're 17 you're a loser!' But the trouble is, while you may realize it's not important to have a boyfriend, it's hard to ignore the pressure to conform.

All my friends have had boyfriends and I haven't. They never excluded me because of that but when they sat down to talk about what it felt like to fancy someone they never bothered to get my opinion because I didn't know anything. When I got a crush on one of my brother's college friends, I was suddenly part of the gang. They always wanted to know if I'd seen him, talked to him on the phone, and how it felt to fancy an older boy.
Susan (15)

This desperation to fall in love and the addictiveness of the feelings associated with it, often leads us to jump in and experiment. However, the prospect can be very frightening and this is when a crush can be useful. A crush allows us to feel those emotions associated with love without actually having to deal with someone. Girls who have crushes describe similar feelings to those who are in love.

WHAT ARE CRUSHES AND WHY DO WE GET THEM?

> Whenever I see him on TV or hear his voice on the radio, my heart jumps, my stomach turns and I get really excited. It's weird, I get this really strange feeling as if he's right in the room. Sometimes, I'll be out and all I really want to do is rush home and watch him on the video. It's almost as if I've got someone at home waiting for me.
> *Yvonne (14)*

What are the symptoms of a crush?

The symptoms of a crush are familiar enough: a drifting in thought and behaviour, a feeling that no one else in life has ever felt this way, and a conviction that this person you love is your ideal mate. Falling into a crush nearly always happens in the same way. You see someone you like and fancy. It could be a boy down the street, a movie star, a pop star, a teacher. You may have seen them before and never given them a second look, but suddenly you begin to feel that this person could be the man for you. Then you start to imagine what this person is like, where they go, what they feel strongly about, etc. At this stage, most people turn into super detectives in their pursuit of information.

> Long before I knew anything about Tom Cruise, I knew he was a lovely man. He's always nice in all his roles and has a really kind face. I didn't really know much about him to begin with so I started buying any magazine with articles about him in it. I've got quite a collection now and I can tell you anything you want to know about him. Who his agent is, what his mother's name is and what he was like at school. I also know where he lives and his likes and dislikes. Reading interviews with him just backs up all the things I've imagined to be true about him.
> *Julia (16)*

Collecting basic information helps to put together a clearer picture of the person and helps us to find out exactly what it is we like about them. It also reaffirms all our fantasies that (1) we've got a lot in common; (2) this makes us right for each other; and (3) if we were in the right situation, we'd go out with them.

> I know people think I'm pathetic to like a pop star but I know if I got the chance to meet him we'd go out. I know I don't know him properly but from what I've read and seen on TV we're very similar. It depresses me because I don't think I'll ever get the chance to meet him and, therefore, I might miss out on going out with someone who is ideal for me.
> *Maggie (16)*

After the initial collection of information, you then start to think about them more and more, using the information you have gleaned. This is when a crush really moves onto a more serious footing, because this is the moment when you start believing that you really know this person. You also become convinced if you had the chance to meet him, he'd fall for you and you'd go out.

> Gavin is a boy who works in my local record shop. He's also in a local band and I always fancied him because we had a lot in common. Once the local paper did a piece on him and I cut it out and put it on my wall because it backed up everything I already thought about him. I spend hours imagining what it would be like to kiss him, to go out with him, what our children would look like and how when he notices me he'd realize how much he loves me. I can't help loving him because he is everything I want from a boyfriend and none of the guys round here match up to that.
> *Sally (17)*

2
The Positive Side of Crushes

Crushes are positive when:

- You feel more happy than unhappy when you think about him.
- The thought of him adds to not subtracts from your life.
- You can laugh about your feelings for him.
- You don't turn down dates because you are saving yourself for him.
- You put your relationship with him in perspective.
- You don't compare every boy you meet to him.
- You don't pin all your hope on him.
- You can see his faults.
- You don't feel completely devastated when you hear he's been out with someone else.
- You don't feel like a lesser person compared to him.
- Your friends know about him.
- You don't talk about him all the time.

The search for love

Everyone wants to fall in love, and not just with any old person. We all want Mr Wonderful, the man who looks just right, acts just right, and says and does all the right things. After all, love is supposed to be the best feeling in the world, isn't it? Look at the movies we watch, the songs we listen to, and the books we read. They are full of tales of love winning against the odds, and of star-crossed lovers fighting to be together through thick and thin. Through these stories, two messages ring out true and strong: being in love is the most unbeatable feeling in the world, and, when it comes to love, anything's possible!

True as these two things may be, the fact is most of us, no

matter how old, are still trying to figure out love's complexities and contradictions. We're all searching for a perfect mate because he or she is supposedly the key to being happy. The problem is, Mr or Mrs Right usually isn't within grabbing distance. Let's face it, sometimes, when you look around, there aren't many people who match up to the image of love's big dream. That boy sitting to your right may be nice but he makes stupid jokes and would rather watch the football than you. As for that guy you work with, he's a known heartbreaker and you don't want to put yourself through that.

The truth is, when it comes to love, none of us want the nasty, hurtful side of it; we all want to fall in love once and make sure it lasts for ever. Of course, we all know that that isn't likely to happen, and that in itself is a scary thought. Most of us would do anything to make sure this doesn't happen, even if it means practising before we jump in. And that's exactly why lots of women pick crushes. After all, it's safer to give something a try in the shallow end than dive straight in.

> I have never fancied any of the guys in my class. They all remind me of my younger brother – spotty, annoying and totally stupid. Their idea of a hot date is to hang about at the shopping centre or play video games. That's not what I want. I'm in love with the actor Keanu Reeves. He's handsome, interesting, and lives the kind of life I want. I know I really won't marry him but I feel like I really know him and that if I met him we'd really get on well. It makes me unhappy sometimes because I may never meet him but most of the time I feel happy because I know he's the kind of man I'll end up with. I hate people who laugh and say, 'It's just a crush'. It may be a crush but I can tell you now I'm sure I have the same feelings as anyone else in love.
> *Amy (15)*

As Amy points out, crushes are very real and not something to be dismissed and smug about. The feelings, the motions and the pain are all very intense and substantial and who is to say that just because it goes on in your mind it doesn't deserve the same attention as other relationships. After all, there's also no getting away from the fact that while you're going through one, it affects your life in every possible way.

First steps into love

The fact is, love and relationships are something we learn about the hard way. It's only by suffering a bit of heartbreak that we learn about what we want and who we want it from. This is why so many people have crushes. They are a safe way of falling into love for the first time, and they get rid of those love-hungry feelings that just eat you up when you're alone and miserable.

Primarily, a crush is very like an everyday relationship; it begins with a physical attraction. You may be watching TV or reading a magazine or sitting on a bus and, before you know it, something catches your attention. Perhaps, it's a hairstyle, the sound of a person's voice, or something he says. Whatever it is, you find yourself thinking of this person every moment of the day. As you find out more and more about him you imagine him to be the perfect person you've been looking for. It's at this stage that your crush really begins.

Before you know it you spend every spare moment of the day imagining what he is doing, where he is, and who he is with. You discover where he goes, who he hangs around with, and the best way you can get to meet him. Then you start thinking what it would be like to go out with him, what he'd say to you and what you'd say to him. Playing out different scenarios in your head helps you to sort out how to start a conversation with someone you like and admire.

David was my friend's older brother. I hardly knew him to speak to but my best friend told me everything about him. I had such a crush on him for two years. He was funny and always made a point to talk to me when I came round. I would

THE POSITIVE SIDE OF CRUSHES

spend hours imagining what I'd say to him, how I'd ask him out and how we'd get together. The truth was I was so shy I hardly ever said a word to him.
Helen (16)

Crushes are very important in helping us go through the motions of love without being hurt. Falling for someone you don't know, and picturing a relationship with all its ups and downs, gives you the equivalent feelings to dating someone. But it is safer, because you don't really get hurt in the same way as an everyday relationship. Mainly because you can change the endings to whatever happens. Many girls admit that it was their crushes that helped them deal with their later relationships. Picturing a possible event and then dealing with it was good practice for the real thing. For instance, you can imagine breaking up without it destroying your life, and then you can imagine making up and getting back together again. You can imagine the worst, that he two-times you, and then visualize how you'd deal with it and how you'd get over it. Playing the same scenario over and over again in your head until you work out the problem satisfactorily is an incredibly useful tool.

Breaking up with my boyfriend hurt so much, especially as I just couldn't get over him. He was on my mind all the time, 24 hours a day, and no one I met ever seemed to match up to him, so I suppose I chose the next best thing. I fell for someone unattainable – a famous singer I'd read about in a magazine. It was a revelation to really fancy someone again and imagine what it would be like to date them. It was a nice safe feeling because I knew I wouldn't ever date this man and, therefore, he could never break my heart. The best thing about it was, it made me realize the qualities I admired in him were ones I wanted in a man and ones my ex-boyfriend never had.
Jill (18)

Let's face it, love makes you feel vulnerable. You put

yourself on the line, open up your heart, and then let the other person know they can hurt you. Not only is this scary, but it's also exhausting. Due to this, some of us subconsciously pick out-of-reach boys because inside we don't feel ready to have a commitment with someone who may let us down. Having a crush is less daunting and far safer; it's rather like watching a preview for a movie. It gives you a little taste of what true love feels like, and how to deal with its complexities, before it actually happens.

> Till I got a crush on an actor I didn't realize how I'd react to being in love. It made me want to stay in alone at nights and stare wistfully at his pictures and watch his films. I ignored my friends and my schoolwork, and lost myself in imagining what our life would be like together. It wasn't until my mum sussed out what was going on that I learned to put my feelings into perspective. She admitted she had felt the same way when she was my age but said that I mustn't give up everything just because of a guy, as it would make me unhappy. So I made myself go out and it helped to take my mind off him. It was a good lesson because now I have a boyfriend and I feel the same way for him as I did for this actor, but now I know not to give up everything for him.
> *Jacqui (16)*

Crushes as an incentive

Strangely enough, most people remember their crushes in more detail than any past relationships. For a lot of people, a crush can work in a very productive and useful way. Many women say their crushes acted as an incentive, a persuasive kick into making them try for something they never dreamed of doing previously. By imagining a better life they realized that anything is possible. After all, deep down inside we all believe that there is someone perfect for us, and, if we're determined that our crush may be the one, then we often push ourselves to do something that will help

THE POSITIVE SIDE OF CRUSHES

it come true. The results often exceed our wildest dreams and our original intentions.

> I've loved Michael Jackson since I was eight years old. I know everything there is to know about him and respect him greatly. Because I wanted to get closer to him I started to get interested in the things he was. I discovered he was into animal rights and so I became a vegetarian and read up on animal campaigns. As I got older I joined a local animal rights group and suddenly realized that I loved working there. From this I am now involved in a big animal charity and work against animal testing. I haven't got a crush on him any more but thanks to him I found my vocation in life.
> *Kelly (18)*

Philippa is a journalist. She decided to become a writer so she could get to meet an actor she had a crush on.

> I had this crush on this actor that lasted for three years. I used to watch his films over and over till my mother got completely sick of me and banned me from watching his films and made me take my posters down. I was so heart-broken but she gave me some sound advice. She said if I was so sure he was the man for me, then I should get off my bottom and do something about meeting him. I figured the best way was to become involved in the same industry, and, as I loved writing, journalism seemed the best option. Of course, I got over my crush a long time ago, but it's thanks to him I'm doing this. Funnily enough, last year I actually got to interview him. He was really nice, and at one stage asked me why I had chosen this career. I told him the truth but I don't think he believed me. It's funny how someone you don't know can change your life.
> *Philippa (21)*

I was in love with my English teacher when I was 14 years old.

THE POSITIVE SIDE OF CRUSHES

My friends told me I had no chance of getting him because he only liked intelligent girls and I wasn't one of them. Partly to prove them wrong, but mainly because I wanted to impress him, I threw myself into my school work. I think I really shocked my parents because from being an average student I actually became good. I have just passed my A levels and am going to university next year, which I'm really happy about. I still have a soft spot for this teacher but at the end of the day he stopped being the reason for my hard work a long time ago.
Hannah (18)

Mark was a boy who played football with my brother. He was dead sporty and very athletic. By comparison, I was one of those girls who always did everything she could to skive off PE. But I was so mad about him that I plotted to get him to notice me and that's how I got into tennis. I was actually quite good at it and started to win local competitions and then county ones. Now I'm planning to go into the national heats next year. Mark and I did go out for a bit because actually being good at something gave me the confidence I had always lacked, and I asked him out. Ironically, I spent so much time at tennis practice that I never had time to see him, so we stopped going out.
Louise (16)

Gary was head of our drama club at school and all my friends had a crush on him. When he started holding auditions for the school play I knew it was a great way to get him to notice me. I didn't get a very big part in his first play, but he was very encouraging and said I could be a good actress if I tried. I suppose that's what made me give acting a real go. Now I'm at drama school and I've had a few TV roles, while Gary gave it all up a long time ago. I don't even know where he is any more. It may sound a pathetic way to get into something you love, but one day when I win an award I'm going to give him a mention and really surprise him.
Cindy (18)

THE POSITIVE SIDE OF CRUSHES

Crushes for fun, confidence, and escapism

Of course, lots of people have crushes just for the sake of them, and why not? They can be fun and very enjoyable. You don't need to have a specific reason for having a crush, and you don't have to do anything when you've got one. Lots of girls jump from one crush to another, replacing one man with another, just for the fun of it.

> I'm the first to admit I have a different crush every week. Last week it was David, a guy I work with on Saturdays; today it's an actor I saw in a film last night. I don't think there's anything wrong with it because I'm not actually hurting anyone. I'm 16 years old and I don't want to tie myself down to a particular boy, so it's far more fun to have crushes and far less trouble.
> *Anna (16)*

Other girls tell of the 'bizarre sense of happiness' their crushes give them – a sense that life isn't as bad as they imagined, and a promise of things to come.

> It may sound ridiculous but sometimes I feel my life is in such a rut. I get up at the same time every day, go to school and then come home, etc., and there seems no end in sight. Having a crush makes my life more exciting. Whenever I'm down I think about him and I feel really happy. I imagine what it would be like to go out with him and the things we'd do. I know it's not real but it's a wonderful way of getting through the more boring parts of my life.
> *Janey (15)*

Older people forget that there is still a tremendous pressure to have a boyfriend. I used to feel inadequate and left out because I didn't know about love. They never included me in their conversations about love because they knew I had never

THE POSITIVE SIDE OF CRUSHES

felt this way about anyone. Then I started liking Tim and, even though I never even spoke to him, suddenly everyone wanted to know my opinions on guys and love.
Wendy (16)

As Wendy has pointed out, the pressure of having to be in a relationship often leads girls to feel alienated and excluded through no fault of their own. A crush alleviates all this and makes you 'part of the gang'.

Despite the popular notion that girls with crushes are giggly, silly, and out of their minds, most girls aren't like this. Knowing a crush isn't real is part of the fascination. It's all pure escapism, designed to give pleasure not despair.

Of course, I know my crush isn't real. I'm never going to meet this man, he's an actor and he lives in Hollywood. If I do ever get there, he'll be married and well out of reach. I do this all for fun. It's exciting to imagine another life in my head. It cheers me up when I'm miserable, and is fun to talk about. Some people get so annoyed when they hear me talk about him. They seem to think I'm being silly and I should pull myself together. But why should I? These are my own fantasies. I don't tell them what to think so I don't see why they feel they can tell me!
Sue (17)

3
The Negative Side of Crushes

Is your crush becoming negative? Try our checklist and see how you rate:

Lack of enthusiasm for life	yes / no
Frequent bouts of unhappiness	yes / no
Feeling of hopelessness	yes / no
Staying in by yourself	yes / no
No motivation to do anything	yes / no
Turning down dates	yes / no
Intense jealousy when others talk about him	yes / no
You think about him *all* the time	yes / no
Feelings of not being 'good enough'	yes / no
Feeling a failure	yes / no

Anyone scoring more than two yeses on this chart needs to take positive action before their crush becomes a depression.

Crushes can be painful

As we've seen, the positive side of crushes can inspire quite life-changing results, but, likewise, the negative side can produce equally devastating effects. Many girls feel guilty about having a crush. They feel that there's something not quite right about the idea of having one, and, hence, something not quite right about themselves. They worry that having a crush means they are weak willed, pathetic, and useless.

> I don't tell too many people about my crush because I know what their reaction will be. They either laugh or tell me to get a life! I know they think I'm stupid and secretly bitch about me behind my back.
> *Lorna (15)*

THE NEGATIVE SIDE OF CRUSHES

Every time I mention I like Cameron, everyone smirks and says, oh not again. You see, he is a famous model and no one I know from round here. My friends all think it's one big joke. One of them even said I should get some professional help because obviously I am crazy to think he'd ever like me.
Joy (14)

Like anything, crushes aren't always exciting and fun; like love, they come with a frustrating and miserable side. They have the power to make you feel depressed, anxious, and downright fed up. Let's face it, the whole business of loving someone is tiring, but a crush is even more exhausting because there's never any physical release from it and no conclusion to all your longing. And, believing you've found the ideal person to love, only to know they are out of reach, is enough to make anyone upset and distraught.

The worst thing about Rob is that I know I'm the right girl for him. The trouble is he doesn't see me enough to realize this. To him I'll always be the little girl who lives next door. It's all so upsetting, we get on so well, but he never gives me a chance. He's going to live in America for a year and I know he's going to fall in love with someone there and then I'll have lost him for ever because of circumstance and nothing else. Whenever I think of this I get so depressed.
Zoe (16)

The fact is, crushes are to do with feelings, and this means they come tied with adverse as well as positive effects. Any thing or person who has the ability to reach down inside you and touch a part that no one else can, brings distress as well as happiness. For some, the distress comes from the realization that nothing concrete can ever happen, while for others the frustration of being so far but so near is too hard to handle.

I dream of Paul every day, I imagine us going out and doing

all the normal things couples do. The truth is he is married and doesn't know I exist. But I know if only he had met me before he met his wife, things would have been so different. When I think of this I get so depressed because it makes my whole life feel hopeless.
Mandy (17)

Living in Never-Never Land is dangerous and depressing. It's no good hoping against all hope that one day you'll just meet your crush, and, lo and behold, he'll fall madly and passionately in love with you. The chances of this happening are minute; no one is saying you and your crush can't make a go of it, but love at first sight is a highly overrated notion. Love takes time to grow, and no amount of wishing can make it appear on the spot. Being madly in love with a pop star/actor/boy across the road is fine, but when you start to believe you're cheated out of a relationship with that person the effects can be devastating. Life suddenly becomes frustrating and unbearable because every moment is spent wishing you were with the man you love at the expense of your everyday life.

I hate that I don't live in LA. I know if I lived there I'd actually bump into him one day. But that's not going to happen here, is it? My life is so boring and dull, one day I'm going to move to America, I know I'll have more chance of going out with him there.
Moira (15)

Cutting yourself off from the world

Crushes are a lot safer for some people than 'real' relationships. They offer a refuge from the hurt and vulnerability of a day-to-day relationship, yet, when you start to cut yourself off from the world, you have to reassess your feelings. Day to day, all our lives are mundane, and even famous people have to deal with the same things as us. No one can escape the trials of normal life.

THE NEGATIVE SIDE OF CRUSHES

Losing yourself in day-dreams is a good way to relax momentarily, but when you find you day-dreams are controlling your life and stopping you from going out then it's time to put things in perspective.

Paula had a crush on a TV soap star for a year:

> It started off as just a laugh, my friends and I would get together and talk about why I'd be a great girlfriend for him. Then I started to really get into him. I knew everything there was to know and would watch his show twice a day and then on video. Finally my friends stopped asking me to go out with them because they knew I'd rather stay at home watching videos and reading magazine articles about him. I remember one time this boy in my class asked me out and I actually said no because I felt it would be unfair to the real person I loved. Also this boy was nothing like the actor I liked. After about a year I suddenly realized that I didn't have many friends left and the ones I did have were always saying that all I ever talked about was this actor. My family were sick of him too, and banned me from watching his videos. I don't know what brought me round to my senses but I think it was the fact that I was actually quite lonely and missed my friends and doing normal everyday things. I still like him but not in the same way. I think I just kind of fell out of love with him and I'm glad.
> *Paula (15)*

Some people purposefully lose themselves in a crush and cut themselves off from everyday life, but for a different reason. These people are perfectionists. They often prefer to place the object of their affections on a pedestal, looking up to everything they do and imagining them to be perfect in every way. In this way, they cut themselves off from having a relationship with anyone else in order to make sure they don't get hurt. They dream about a person endlessly, but no one else can possibly meet their image of perfection. Even the person on the pedestal can't stay up there forever and will eventually come crashing down, causing more disappointment and upset.

David was the perfect man to me. He was funny, charming, older than me, and had a great job. All the boys I knew were nothing like that. When I first liked him, I was going out with Rob, but I could see that Rob would never be like David. I eventually ditched Rob, and my friends thought I was stupid, but it was David I wanted. I hardly knew him but I knew we were right for each other. Then, after about three months of fancying him from afar, I got my chance with him. Unfortunately, he was nothing like I imagined him to be, he was rude, stroppy, and a real flirt. I threw away a good relationship for someone I didn't even know.
Becky (16)

I know I've cut myself off from having a relationship but that's because I suppose I don't really want one right now. Having a crush is like having a relationship without all the hassle and hurt. My crush is the ideal boyfriend, he does what I want, he behaves the way I want, and I know he'll never leave me for another girl and hurt me like some of my boyfriends. I suppose when I'm ready I'll fall for someone 'real', but until then I'm quite happy to spend time alone with my day-dreams.
Jan (17)

Being realistic

Unrequited love is the most heart-breaking love of all. It can destroy your life and your self-confidence if you let it. If your school work is suffering, your friends washing their hands of you, and your family pulling out their hair, just because of your crush, then you have to learn to put it into perspective. Being realistic doesn't mean you have to give up on your day-dreams and forego all crushes for the rest of your life. All it means is that you have to

THE NEGATIVE SIDE OF CRUSHES

designate time for your crush and time for the rest of your life. Becoming lovesick and depressed is not what crushes are about. So try to follow these eight rules to stop your crush from becoming negative:

1 Don't mistake lust for love.

For many people, the first instance of a crush is a physical one. You see a person, maybe on a train, on TV, or at the cinema. Suddenly this person becomes the one you've been looking for all your life. He is beautiful and you know you're meant to be together because it feels like love. STOP! Remember, lust feels similar, but real love involves a growing and strengthening relationship. This means communication, and how can you really communicate with someone you don't know? Love also comes from mutual respect, and you can't have this if you've never met someone.

> I have to keep reminding myself that I put posters on my wall because he looks nice in them and not because I know him. It's funny isn't it, how you can look at a person's picture and think that means you really know them. I look at his facial features and I think that's why I like him, that's why he's such a nice person. But at the end of the day, I know the posters are there because I fancy his looks, and nothing else.
> *Paula (14)*

2 You don't really know them.

Okay, so you've read everything they've ever said, or interrogated someone who really knows them. But think of things from a different angle. If someone spoke to all your friends, looked at your picture, watched you on the street, and read all about your past, would they really know you? Of course, they wouldn't. They would have a fairly good idea about you, but they wouldn't even get near the real you. Learning about people from other sources is useful, but it still only gives you a two-dimensional view. To understand and know a person you have to meet them on a one-to-one basis.

> A year ago if you'd asked me if I knew Michael, I would have said yes. After all, I knew what he liked, where he went, and who he hung out with. I also knew most of his ex-girlfriends. I thought I was quite an expert on him, but I really wasn't. I saw him at a party one day and he was snogging this girl in the kitchen while his girlfriend was in the other room. That really woke me up. I thought 'what a creep'. He may have all those good qualities but he's a creep underneath it all.
> *Anna (16)*

3 Write down a list of positive and negative things about your crush.

Include things like where you both live, ages, and interests. Then see if you're really that compatible with him. If he's your teacher, then you're never going to have a relationship with him because it would be unethical. If he's dating your best friend, he's not suddenly going to change his mind. How out of reach is your crush? Be honest with yourself, because it will save you a lot of heart-break in the long run.

> I had a crush on my sister's boyfriend for a year. He was such a flirt and liked the fact that I liked him. But I had to stop myself from going near him because I knew what would happen if my crush became real. It would never have worked out and my sister and family would never have forgiven me.
> *Louise (15)*

4 Set aside certain times of the day to think about him.

Most of us day-dream constantly. Apart from being fun it's a great way to escape some of the more tiresome aspects of our lives. However, if you find yourself drifting in and out of conversations, forgetting where you're going and missing school, then you've got a problem. You need to fight the

THE NEGATIVE SIDE OF CRUSHES

temptation to let your mind wander. It may be hard at first, but you can do it. Day-dreaming is just a habit, and like all habits it can be broken. This means concentrating on what you're doing by bargaining with yourself. For instance, you can make yourself pay attention in class by promising yourself time alone at home to day-dream. There's plenty of time during the day to day-dream, for example, in the bath, on the way to school, before you go to sleep, etc., without giving up on anything important.

> At one stage my teachers called my mum up to the school, because they wondered if I had a problem at home. You see, I had been in the top class all year but since I got a crush on this actor, I stopped even caring about my work. My mum knew exactly what I'd been doing and went mad. She said I had to show her all my homework before I could even go near the TV and video. We argued like crazy, but that was the only way she could get me to see how obsessed I was becoming.
> *Philippa (14)*

5 Don't drive yourself crazy and put yourself down.

We all have negative thoughts about ourselves and crushes sometimes bring these out even more. If we really scrutinize ourselves, we can come up with a hundred things that are wrong. For instance, we're either too fat or too thin, too tall or too short. We've got frizzy hair when we want straight hair; the list is endless. The fact is, these are just excuses to stop ourselves from liking what we've got. If you use these as reasons why your crush doesn't fancy you, then you are crazy. Beauty really is in the eye of the beholder and what you find attractive someone else may loathe, so don't use this is a reason why your crush is out of reach.

> Every time I saw Keith out with a girl I'd go home, look at myself in the mirror, and find a hundred reasons why he hadn't asked me out. It was always that I wasn't pretty and thin

THE NEGATIVE SIDE OF CRUSHES

enough. I kept thinking if only I was thin, then he'd like me. I dieted like crazy for a while and became way too thin and ill. Of course, he still didn't ask me out and the next time I saw him, he was dating this big girl. That made me laugh and realize how stupid I was being. I knew then the real reason he didn't ask me out was because he didn't even know me.
Pam (16)

6 Don't bore your friends stupid with stories about him.

Falling in love with someone is always interesting to the two people involved, but unfortunately not for their friends. It's tempting to talk about someone you like and admire, but while your friends might be interested at first, in the long run they'll tire very quickly of the subject. Think about it this way: if your friend was into fly fishing, and loved it, how kindly would you take to having to watch videos of it, hear anecdotes, and generally be made to sit and listen to facts about it? Not very kindly, I'll bet. So, remember, the less you talk about your crush the more sympathetic your friends will be when you do feel the need to bring the subject up.

> My poor friends, when I think what I've put them through. One friend came to that same record shop with me every night for four months, just so I could watch a guy who worked behind the counter. Another sat while I watched the same music video over and over for three hours. I'm surprised they still talk to me.
> *Helen (15)*

7 Don't compare every living man you meet to him.

Remember what we said about pedestals and how they come crashing down? Well, no one's perfect, not even your crush. You have faults and so does everyone else. Sometimes, we restrict ourselves by making it clear we're not interested in anything else. It's okay to have a crush but it's not okay to stop dating because

THE NEGATIVE SIDE OF CRUSHES

you're saving yourself for him. After all, you can still go out and have fun without ruining your day-dreams.

> I didn't have a boyfriend for four years because of my crushes. I'd jump from one famous person to another, thinking, 'God, I wish I had a real boyfriend so I didn't have to make do with a crush'. I didn't realize that my crushes were stopping me from even looking interested in any other boy. I mean, who could live up to Richard Gere or Keanu Reeves? Not anyone I knew.
> *Sue (20)*

8 Have a good think about why your crush came about.

Was it because you had a really bad relationship and this is helping you overcome it? Or is it because you want to be in love? Is it their glamorous life you admire rather than them? Try and work out why you like this person. Is it because he has all the attributes you admire, or because he's famous/older/in authority? Often, working out the reason behind a crush can make it easier to bear.

Kelly had a crush for three years on her teacher:

> My crush made me so unhappy for such a long time, until I realized why I liked Mr Rogers so much. He reminded me of my Dad who died when I was five years old. I think I started to really miss my dad when I started senior school, and Mr Rogers was the first teacher who was nice to me when I started that school. He was also young and very kind to me in a way that no other teacher had ever been. And I think I read that to be something it wasn't. Now I've realized that, I can like him for being a good teacher and nothing more.
> *Kelly (15)*

Crying, talking, and seeking help

So, what if you do all these things and still you feel like your

THE NEGATIVE SIDE OF CRUSHES

world is caving in and everything is pointless? Well, you now have to take some positive action. This means talking about how you feel and getting all your pent up fears, emotions, and anxieties out into the open, so they don't drive you crazy.

Crying is a great release and can get rid of frustration and despair in one fell swoop. Crying about your crush isn't pathetic or a weakness. It's a great release and will make you feel a hundred times better. Love and crushes are hard to cope with and crying is sometimes the easiest way out of feeling down. Sometimes, we want to cry and just can't release the tears; if this is your problem, try settling down with a slushy video or writing down how you feel. Learning to relax can also help the tears to come out. Try lying on your back and taking deep breaths, till you feel more in control.

It can also help to talk to your friends about the down side of your crush. By this I don't mean bore them with anecdotes and stories, but tell them how upset you're feeling. People often underestimate the extent to which their friends and family are upset, because we are all very good at hiding our true feelings. Having a crush is a very private thing and while this is one of its pluses, it can also be a very negative experience. Keeping everything to yourself gives your problems an air of importance that can blow things out of proportion. Living everything, both good and bad, in your head can make you feel like you're going crazy. However, if you share your feelings, you'll be less likely to suffer from the depressing side-effects of a crush, and it will help to keep your feet safely on the ground.

Of course, talking about your feelings isn't always easy, but if you confide in someone you love and trust, they aren't going to laugh at you or turn you away. Given half a chance, many people will be just as sympathetic to unrequited love as they are to an everyday relationship. In any case, you don't have to tell them who the person is, if you want to keep it private or feel they really won't understand. If you're someone who isn't used to talking about yourself, then start by writing down how you feel. Remember, no one is going to see your efforts, and if you can't

THE NEGATIVE SIDE OF CRUSHES

bring yourself to reread them, then fine, but don't underestimate the power of talking.

> I used to have really bad trouble sleeping at night. I'd wake up thinking of Chris and all the reasons why he wouldn't date me. Then one night I was so upset I sat down and wrote a letter to him. I never had any intention of sending it to him, I just wrote it as if I would send it. I said everything I wanted to say to him, how I felt, how much I loved him and why I thought we'd be good together, then I fell asleep straight away. In the morning I ripped it up, but now when I can't sleep I write to him and I find I feel less upset and anxious.
> *Karen (16)*

If you really have no one to confide in, Karen's solution might be the ideal one for you. If not, there are a number of agencies who can help and advise you. After all, a problem shared is a problem halved. The Samaritans (number in your local directory) are on hand to offer a listening ear at any time of the day or night. They won't judge you, but will offer you sympathy and understanding. Childline and Careline are two organizations that can also offer you free advice and confidential counselling. Their numbers are in the Useful Addresses section at the end of this book.

Finally, remember, crushes are supposed to be fun. If you find you're crying more than you're laughing, you're depressed more than you're happy, and your everyday life doesn't match up to your fantasy life, then it's time to seek help. As alone as you may feel, there are people who can help: friends, family, teachers, your doctor, and the above organizations. Whatever you do, you don't have to suffer alone.

4
Crushes on Famous People

A famous woman once said 'Crushes are a rehearsal for orgasm!' As true as this may be, anyone who has ever plastered their bedroom walls with a hundred grinning posters, queued in the rain for a glimpse of their beloved, or wasted hours just staring into space imagining *the* moment when your eyes will lock across a crowded arena, knows that loving a famous person is not just about sex. It's about a desire to live a life that's a million miles away from your present one. It also has a lot to do with glamour, competing with your friends, dealing with jealousy, and getting the ultimate man of your fantasies to fall in love with plain old you.

Of course, who you get a crush on varies from person to person, but the majority of crushes on famous people fall into two categories: pop stars and actors. You can have a crush on anyone, and sometimes the most unlikely candidate can become the object of your affections.

> I fell in love with a guy in a Madonna video. I only had one article on him that I found in a woman's magazine, but I used to watch the video over and over for about three months. I actually liked the fact that he wasn't very famous and hardly anyone knew him. It made me think a meeting and subsequent relationship was more likely. It's only when I heard a girl at college talk about him and heard other girls fancied him that I realized it wasn't very likely at all.
> *Karen (16)*

> My crush was on an American film star. He lived in LA, was married and ten years older than me. This didn't stop me from becoming completely fixated by him. I had posters of him all over the walls, knew every detail about him and convinced

CRUSHES ON FAMOUS PEOPLE

myself that the day I got to LA he'd bump into me walking down the street and we'd fall in love.
Kath (15)

As Kath points out, sometimes the less likely love is, the more strongly you feel, because it makes you believe more firmly the love you have is unique. And the more fantasies you play through in your head, the more you believe you've found your ideal partner. Talk to anyone who has a crush and you'll find they leave nothing to chance. All their fantasies are minutely plotted and laid out. Alice is a 15-year-old fan of a popular TV star. She talks constantly of how she'll change her name to her crush's name, have his baby, and then be there for him when he's no longer a star. Another 15-year-old, Sunni, insists her friends join in with her fantasy scenarios.

> I like to play different possibilities over and over again, until the slightest crease is ironed out, just in case I ever meet him and we get together.
> *Sunni (15)*

Even if crushes on famous people (especially pop stars) aren't as old as some other crushes, they certainly have had more impact upon teenagers in the last 40 years than anything else. The so-called crush phenomenon started in the 1950s with Frank Sinatra, and has carried on in the same way to this day. In fact, the way the media has dealt with pop stars and their fans is partly responsible for why crushes are dealt with so unsympathetically. Take the way the newspapers dealt with Sinatra in the 1950s and The Beatles in the 1960s.

The US papers dubbed Sinatra the 'National Teenage Love Affair' and the papers went on to record: 'Girls ran screaming down the road after him, bought his records by the bucket full and pinned pictures everywhere. The frenzy of his fans has left the general public totally bemused.' Ten years later people were explaining The Beatles phenomenon as 'escapism', 'substitution

CRUSHES ON FAMOUS PEOPLE

for love', 'teenage hysteria' and 'a necessary spontaneous emotion'. But as one fan now confesses:

> My behaviour wasn't that spontaneous. It had more to do with the fact that I thought I loved them. I would practise how to behave when I saw them by putting on their records in my room and standing around and weeping for a while. Then the song would end and I'd fall to the floor exhausted. I'd also practise kissing my hand and pillow, just in case one of them ever asked me for a kiss. That's the only thing that came in handy later on.
> *Jane (45)*

Other girls specialize in pop star crushes because of the camaraderie their crushes bring. The feeling that they are somehow part of the gang, that even if no one they know understands how they feel, at least some other girls do.

> I do get jealous when I see other girls mad about him. But it's nice to have friends who like him because it helps when you get depressed and miserable. It makes you realize you're not alone and that everyone feels despondent now and then. And I know feeling this way is just all part of it.
> Rebecca (14)

Winning the man of your dreams against the odds not only seems romantic, but it's exciting and passionate as well. Yet, the downside of a crush on a famous person is as demoralizing as any other crush. If the person of your dreams lives a thousand miles away, then the fact is he isn't just going to plop into your life one day. Even if he lives in the same country as you, his busy schedule and life-style doesn't exactly make him accessible to you. Of course, none of this helps if you are currently baffled at why you feel so miserable and frustrated. Love is supposed to be happy and fun, and yet crushes often seem to have the exact opposite effect.

CRUSHES ON FAMOUS PEOPLE

How to cope with a crush on a famous person

1 Keep it fun.
Remember way back when you first started liking him, remember what fun it all was: collecting snippets of information about him, discovering new facts, watching things you hadn't seen him on, listening to interviews; talking with your friends, laughing about him? When did it all go sour? Probably when you started wishing you could really go out with him. When you realised you both had a lot in common, and when you realized you'd only got a chance in a million of reaching him.

> I cry every night because I know I can't get near him. Once I found out a hotel his band was staying at, and arrived there only to find 500 other fans with the same idea. I was so upset I went home in tears. I waited all year to see him in concert, but was so unhappy all the way through because I knew this would be the only time I'd ever see him in the flesh.
> *Susan (16)*

You have to remember that crushes are supposed to be fun. If he's a pop star he wants you to enjoy his music not be sad about it; if he's a film star he'd be mortified to see you so upset at something that's supposed to be entertainment. Your crush is your own private relationship, so don't make it a miserable experience. You can make it into anything you want and no one will ever know. You can imagine the silly things you'd do, how he'd kiss you, what you'd call your children, and you need never be embarrassed because no one will ever know. You're not hurting anyone, you're not mad, and you're doing nothing wrong.

The step from plain fantasizing into really believing is easy to do. So, make sure you ground yourself firmly: read interviews

CRUSHES ON FAMOUS PEOPLE

with your crushes, pin posters up and watch their films; but make sure you always say to yourself 'I'm doing this because it's fun, and I watch you because I like the way you look. I don't really know you and you don't really know me.' It may be hard at first, but it will make you realize that you can still like him without him ruling your life.

2 Set aside a time in the day to dream about him.

Hands up who spends all their time day-dreaming about their crushes? Well, if you're being honest, all your hands will be up. The fact is, like love, crushes get to a stage when all you can do is think about them. You fall asleep and they're on your mind, you wake up and there they are again, you sit in lessons and all you can hear is their voice. It's all a very normal stage of a relationship, but the fact is it's also very disruptive.

> I rarely go out any more because I like to sit in my room and listen to my tapes and stare at a picture of him. My friends say I should go out more, and even my mum gets annoyed with me. Can't they see I'm happy, I don't need anyone but him?
> *Lindy (16)*

It's easy to think like Lindy, but the trouble is you do need other people, if not to wake you up to 'real' life, then to be there when you realize a picture is no real company. Some girls find that day-dreaming their life away has more direct effects.

> My schoolwork has really gone down the toilet. I can't concentrate on anything.
> *Lucy (13)*

> I can't eat a thing. I feel sick whenever I think about him.
> *Julie (17)*

> I feel sad all the time. Like my heart's breaking.
> *Sam (15)*

CRUSHES ON FAMOUS PEOPLE

As you can see, imagined relationships can cause as much heartache as real ones, in fact sometimes more, because people aren't that sympathetic. If you feel like this, there is a way out, and that's to discipline yourself. Limit yourself to certain times a day when you can think about him. Maybe just before you go to bed or after you've had dinner. That way your crush will feel more exciting and you won't be ruining the rest of your life.

3 Don't make yourself mad with jealousy.

> I used to get so mad whenever another girl in my class said she liked him, because I liked him first and I felt she was trying to take him away from me. I'd end up having a really big fight about it. Now I realize that he isn't mine to hold on to and, though that's sad, it's helping me to get over him.
> *Sam (15)*

No one wants to think that they have to compete for their dream man. On top of this, no one wants to believe that anyone else could understand him as well as they do. Realizing this isn't true, is hard to deal with. It makes you confront emotions you probably haven't had to deal with before, like jealousy, envy, hate, and despair. These are the downsides to love, and learning to cope with them will help you greatly when you have a real relationship.

> When I heard he was getting married I felt like he was two-timing me and I hated her. She was so pretty, a real model type. I kept thinking she was after his money and even thought about writing a letter to warn him. Now, years later, I can see how ridiculous I was being, and I even quite like her. It's a bit like getting over an ex and learning to cope with his new girlfriend.
> *Donna (19)*

If you feel yourself wrought with jealousy over other fans, tell yourself that these girls are in exactly the same position as you.

CRUSHES ON FAMOUS PEOPLE

Of course, they don't feel exactly the same way as you do because your relationship is unique, but they do understand what you are going through. Talk to them and you may find yourself with a new friend.

> Two of the best friends I ever made were eight years ago when I used to follow this pop band around. One of the guys was my hero and I adored him. I'd wait outside hotels and stay around till 12 am. I never talked to the other girls because I felt they didn't know the band like me and I felt in competition with them. Then one night this girl and her friend started talking to me and I realized I'd been wrong. They were just like me. It helped me to get a better perspective on what I was feeling and I ended up making two great friends.
> *Lisa (23)*

4 Don't feel you are being cheated out of a relationship with him.

This is a hard one. After all, when everything feels right and the only thing that stands between you and him is a couple of thousand miles, his life-style, and a girlfriend, it's easy to think you're being cheated. After all, why would you have been led towards him if it wasn't to have a relationship?

The fact is, crushes happen for a number of reasons, sometimes to teach us how to handle love, other times to help us get over a broken heart or protect us from getting one. Making yourself believe you have been cheated will only lead to more misery.

> I felt for years it was my parents' fault. If only they were richer, or more trendy, then I'd have a chance to meet him. Then it became if only I'd been born in America, or if only I could act and be discovered. It was romantic in a sick kind of way. I kept imagining if only I could get over all these stumbling blocks we'd be together for ever. Finally I realized

CRUSHES ON FAMOUS PEOPLE

they weren't really stumbling blocks but reasons why we wouldn't be compatible in real life.
Janey (18)

5 Don't let anyone tell you imagined relationships aren't painful.

There are thousands of people right now suffering heartache over someone who doesn't love them back. Most of their desires don't love them back because they don't even know the person who has fallen in love with them. Frustration is the most unbearable part of a crush; frustration at not getting what you want, at trying and not succeeding, and frustration at being laughed at for having feelings.

> I often wonder if he gives any thought to girls like me who are madly in love with him. I doubt it. He probably is too worried about his own life.
> *Kelly (15)*

> No one is very sympathetic. They just laugh when I tell them why I am so sad, some say pull yourself together, others think I'm slightly crazy. But I don't see what's wrong with loving someone from afar. And I don't think I deserve to be ridiculed.
> *Jenny (15)*

The important thing to remember is that the feelings you're experiencing are very real, whether they are good or bad. You can't snap out of being unhappy in the same way you can't snap out of being happy. Learning to deal with the root of your problem is the best way to come to terms with it. For a start, try and work out why you feel so heart-broken. Is it because you know there's no hope or no chance that your dream will become a reality? The next step is to be honest with yourself. Are you deluding yourself into thinking there's a possible relationship when there isn't? You have the right to be miserable if you've

CRUSHES ON FAMOUS PEOPLE

come to these conclusions, but don't punish yourself for ever about it. Pick yourself up, and tell yourself someone real is waiting just round the corner for you. As 24-year-old Alice points out, it was only when she let go of her three-year crush on a film star that she met a man who turned out to be the one she fell in love with.

> The fact is, when you give up pinning all your hopes and dreams on someone who isn't real, and letting go of what your life together could have been. You make space for a 'real' person and you realize, so what if he's not perfect, a film star, or anything else? He's wonderful and that's all that matters.

No one deserves to be ridiculed for having feelings and if you feel downright miserable, unhappy and/or suicidal, then you need to find someone to talk to. If your family laugh off your worries, then there are other people who will listen and help you. Childline (phone 0800 1111) are on hand 24 hours a day to talk through your worries. Don't let anyone make you think you're imagining it.

6 *Talk, but don't overdo it.*

It's very easy when you fall in love to think the person you've fallen for is the most interesting, sexy, intelligent person you've ever met, and they may be, but only to you. There's nothing worse than having to sit through endless hours of the same conversation about the same person. So don't bore your friends. Sure, talk about your crush, but if you go on and on they'll soon get bored of you.

> Anna is so sad. She just talks about this pop star all the time. She even calls herself his wife and talks about where they'll live and what they'll do. It was quite funny at first but now it's so boring. She's never interested in what we think or like. Whenever I bring my boyfriend she compares him to her

make-believe one. I feel like saying, you idiot, at least mine's real. She drives me mad.
Sally (15)

If this sounds like a description of you, it's time to wake up. Crushes are very boring to other people, so make sure you don't witter on and on about them. Of course, if you need someone to talk to if you get miserable, then your friends are the ones to turn to, but they won't be there if you've bored them stiff over months and months. Keep the good things about your crush to yourself, that way no one will ridicule you, you'll have your own private affair, and no one can put a damper on how you feel.

7 Be realistic.
Your crush is part based on what the person looks like, what you've read or heard about them, and not what you actually know from being face to face with them. The fact is, people in the flesh are very different from how you imagine them to be. For instance, if someone had a picture of you, read your biography, saw you on video, then convinced themselves you were the one for them, you'd think it a bit strange wouldn't you?

The definition of a fantasy is 'a fanciful invention or speculation'. This means the image you have of the person you love can't by any stretch of the imagination be true. After all, in our fantasies, dream men are always nice, always come back and always love us; in reality no one can live up to such high expectations. Of course, you can get a vague idea what they're like from interviews, but even this is misleading. For a start, most magazines won't print the horrible stuff (if there is any), he will be warned about what he's going to be asked, and he isn't going to tell the complete truth. Public images are very important to famous people and they do their utmost to make sure their images stay clean and pure. As you're never getting the whole picture, you're never going to be really sure of who the person is you like and admire.

So save yourself a lot of heart-break: don't put your crush on a

CRUSHES ON FAMOUS PEOPLE

pedestal; remember, not only is he human, but he is fallible as well. He makes mistakes, gets angry and probably has crushes too.

> It was really strange reading an interview with him. He was talking about having a crush on an old pop star and he described exactly how I was feeling. It was so weird, but it made me realize he was a real person and did the same things as you and me. And this helped me to get over him.
> *Beccy (15)*

The following girls all went one step further and met their crushes. This is how their dream man matched up to the real man:

> I won a competition to meet him and was early. I walked in with my friend and I saw him screaming at some woman about having to meet more silly fans. I went right off him there and then. He was really embarrassed and apologized but that didn't help.
> *Gail (16)*

> I met him at the airport, I was with my mum waiting for the same plane as him. I went up to him and he was so nice, really kind and made me laugh. He talked to me for ten minutes, gave me an autograph and had his picture taken with me. I went away thinking I was completely right about him. Later, I went back to ask him if he'd write to me and I heard him doing exactly the same thing with another girl. I was heart-broken but I could hardly blame him. It's his job and I'd forgotten that.
> *Sam (15)*

> I had the time of my life when I met him after a concert, but I didn't think he'd drink or smoke and he did both. He also made people run around and get things for him, and that put

me off slightly. Also I asked him about things he'd said in interviews that had touched me and he couldn't remember saying any of them.
Lee (16)

8 Don't cut yourself off from the boys you know.

Okay, so that spotty oik you sit next to has none of the charms of Tom Cruise. He can't sing like a pop star and has no sense of dress, but that's not his fault. Anyway, who knows what he could turn out to be if only you gave him a chance.

> I just don't fancy any of the boys I know. They are all stupid and insensitive. One guy just asked me out and I said no, he's okay but I fancy a pop star and I can't bring myself to date someone ordinary while I still like him. I kind of feel I am being unfaithful to him, I know it sounds stupid and I don't think I'll ever go out with my crush, but I won't go out with anyone who doesn't live up to him.
> *Rebecca (14)*

The important thing to remember is every famous man was a spotty oik at some point in his life. So, imagine all those girls who are kicking themselves now because they ignored what was under their noses. The boys around you also have one advantage your crush doesn't have: they are right here in the flesh. After all, you can't go to a party with a poster, and you can't really kiss someone on a video screen. Life with a crush can be exciting and glamorous but after a while it can also be lonely and disappointing.

> Sometimes, I get really miserable, I feel like no one understands how I feel. I think about how I feel and the fact that he doesn't know I'm alive, and it really hurts. But I've never met anyone whom I fancy like him.
> *Cara (15)*

CRUSHES ON FAMOUS PEOPLE

A famous old song goes 'He's not the man I've been dreaming of, but he's sure the man I love'. What this song tries to point out is that it's okay to dream and fantasize but, sometimes, happiness is right in front of you, if only you'd open your eyes. Anyway, even if a boy who fancies you isn't the man of your dreams, you have to realize the man of your dreams isn't that person either. As supermodel Cindy Crawford once said about herself, 'Even I don't look like Cindy Crawford at home.'

Having been a journalist for many years and met many a famous man, I've realized two things: one, they're always shorter than you think, and, two, they never look like their pictures. Why? Well, simply because they have a team of people paid to make them look wonderful. Imagine if the boys in your class had someone to do their hair and make-up, a stylist who picked all their clothes and dressed them, a photographer paid to make them look attractive, a manager who told them what to say, a speech expert who refined their accents, and someone to help them look fit and healthy. Wouldn't they all look like superstars too?

> I like him because of what he says in interviews. He's really funny, and sensitive. He always talks about the kind of girl he wants to date and I'm very like her. He also writes these songs that seem really personal for him, and they are personal for me as well. That's why I know we'd be really good together.
> *Helen (15)*

Of course, looks aren't the only thing that attracts us to a famous person. Sometimes, with actors, it can be a specific role they play or have played, and, with pop stars, a cause they believe in or a song that hits a specific personal note. While this can be a good start for a 'normal' relationship, it is not very practical when you don't know someone. The reality is, most famous people are not within reach and, no matter how much you think you can make a relationship happen, you can't. Therefore, just because Mr X says something that sounds as if he'd get on wonderfully with

CRUSHES ON FAMOUS PEOPLE

you, it doesn't equal that he's the man for you. In an ideal situation you may be right, but when he lives miles away, and doesn't even know you exist, the odds aren't on your side.

5
Crushes on Older Men

He's smooth, he's charming, he has a car, he has money, he's perfect, but he's at least ten years older than you, if not more. Still, so what? Age doesn't matter when you're in love, does it? Unfortunately, when you're under 18 it does. Maybe not to you, but definitely to him, your parents, and everyone else you know. Which, let's face it, on the one hand makes him even more interesting, sexy, and worth pursuing.

The fact is, crushes on older men are bad news, apart from the little details, like the object of your desires is probably married, engaged or has a girlfriend. Whether you like it or not, he is in a completely different league from you. Pursuit is at the very core of most crushes, and when this pursuit is aimed at famous people or people your own age, it's very easy to get carried away. After all, you can quiz your girlfriends about that boy at school, buy magazines about that actor, but you can't let yourself get carried away like this over an older man. Asking around about an older guy is dangerous because it won't be long before someone gets a whiff of what you're up to. When this happens, the chances are this someone may not understand what you're doing and before you know it a rumour has started. This then leads to things getting out of hand, accusations flying around, and people being hurt.

If you're presently in the midst of a crush on an older man there are a few realities you should face up to before you get hurt or hurt the other person.

CRUSHES ON OLDER MEN

Why you like him and why it is dangerous

1 You're likely to make life very difficult for the person you have a crush on if you constantly hang around.

The suspicion is likely to fall on him, not you, and while you may enjoy it, it's likely to effect your crush's life. Take 15-year-old Helen who had a crush on 28-year-old Nick.

> Two years ago I was in love with a 28-year-old guy who worked at the local cafe where I had a Saturday job. I knew he had a girlfriend but I really liked him. He flirted with me, he was funny, and I'd never met anyone like him before. Once the manager told me to leave him alone because everyone thought he was having an affair with me. I was only 15 years old and didn't care what people thought.
> *Helen (17)*

I'm the kind of person who likes to have a laugh with everyone. I suppose I was stupid but I didn't realize Helen fancied me, I mean I was 13 years older than her. The first I heard about it was when my manager at work gave me a talking to. Apparently Helen had been telling people how well we got on and how much she liked me. He warned me she was under age and that shocked me because I had no intention of getting involved with her. My girlfriend wasn't pleased either, and in the end I had to just stop talking to Helen which I think hurt her very much, but I had to protect myself.
Nick (30)

2 You're unlikely ever to get much out of this relationship, even if you got it together with this man.

The chances are he'll never see you as an equal. Problems such as what you like doing and what different things he wants to do are bound to arise.

CRUSHES ON OLDER MEN

After three years of having a crush on Steve we finally went out together. He was 23 years old, only six years older than me but you'd have thought it was 40 the way he went on. I was always wrong in his eyes and always stupid. We broke up after two months and I was heart-broken. He wasn't the man I dreamed he'd be.
Gail (17)

The age difference never seems much when you're dreaming about it. It's just not a problem. In reality it is a huge one. When I finally started seeing Gary, the ten years between us became even bigger. None of our friends got on, we didn't like doing the same things and had completely different tastes.
Sue (17)

3 If you do finally get to go out with him, he is bound to be more sexually active than you, and will expect more than you can give.

Also, by the nature of your ages, everyone will assume he's up to something and will want to take advantage of you.

This girl told everyone she was in love with me and I hardly knew her. It turned out she lived at the end of my road and was 13! I was 18 at the time, so you can imagine how well that went down. She told her friends I slept with her, her parents found out, and came round ready to report me to the police. Of course, I'd never said a word to her, but it was hard to prove it. Finally, she just confessed she'd been joking. Some joke. She nearly got me arrested.
Stuart (19)

4 While you focus on him, no boy your own age will ever live up to his image.

After all, they have bags more confidence than the boys your age, which makes them more attractive straight away. They aren't afraid to approach you, talk to you, make you laugh.

CRUSHES ON OLDER MEN

I know exactly why I like my brother's best friend. He is unlike any of the boys I know. He's clever and funny and not afraid to talk about love and things like that. He's always telling me about how his ex-girlfriend broke his heart and things like that. My last boyfriend lasted one day because he hardly even said five words the whole night we were together.
Ollie (15)

5 Older men seem more supportive and able to offer security and stability than younger men.

Ask any woman in her mid twenties if this is true and she'll probably laugh in your face. The fact is, age doesn't bring maturity, experience does. From the outside it can look as if a person is mature, but clothes and money don't equal security.

Frankie was my sister's ex-boyfriend and I'd always had a crush on him because he seemed like the ideal boyfriend. He was always looking after my sister, buying her things, taking her everywhere, and being sweet. I couldn't understand why she dumped him. It's only when he kept calling up to speak to me, that she told me the truth. He was horribly possessive and wouldn't let her go anywhere with her friends, or wear sexy clothes, and even made a fuss about make-up. It's only when she pointed this out that I began to see that he wasn't the person I thought he was.
Fiona (14)

6 Your friends will be impressed.

You may baulk at this one, but the truth is, having an older boyfriend scores points off your friends. And making them believe something is going on when it isn't can give you sudden credibility.

My music teacher was a student at the local college. I had a really bad crush on him and part of it came from knowing my friends would be jealous if I told them about him. They

wanted to believe as badly as I did that he fancied me, so I exaggerated everything. Then one day I bumped into him on the street with my friends and I was so embarrassed because he was with someone who was obviously his girlfriend. I felt so humiliated, but it was my own fault. I let my dreams get out of control.
Gill (14)

The most dangerous older man to have a crush on – a teacher

Teachers are often in the front line when it comes to crushes because they are so accessible. It's easy to talk to them, see them, find out information about them, and basically day-dream while they are right in front of you. Many teachers start off as role models and then this can gradually progress to a crush. It's okay to have a crush on a teacher as long as you don't make it obvious. It's a safe way to feel in love and can even put some excitement into a dreary school day.

I used to hate English until the day our new teacher arrived. He was called Mr Berkeley and was really trendy. He had long hair, little round glasses and didn't talk down to us. I fell in love with him straight away and after that I worked really hard to get his attention. Somewhere along the line I discovered I really liked English and I'm now making a living from it. I don't know where he is now but I'd like to thank him.
Justine (21)

A harmless crush on a teacher can become harmful in two ways. Some teachers will welcome your adoration, but at the same time will have no intention of letting it get out of hand. However, there are a very few bad ones who may try to take advantage of you, and their motive is sexual. If a teacher tries to get involved with you and tells you not to worry, things will work

CRUSHES ON OLDER MEN

out, don't believe him. He is trying to exploit you and you'd do best to stay well clear no matter how much you like him.

> I really liked this teacher until the day he started teasing me about my feelings and stroking my hair. It was after class and I was by myself and suddenly I started to feel really scared. I realized I didn't actually want to have an affair with him, I just wanted to be in love with him. I mumbled something about him being wrong and ran out. He hasn't spoken to me since.
> *Elaine (16)*

If a teacher continues to harrass you and won't leave you alone, then tell your parents and friends what's going on. Make sure you're never alone with him and note down everything he says and does to you. This way you'll have back-up evidence when you report him. It doesn't matter how much you've fantasized about him, talked about him, or found out about him, it isn't reason enough for him to exploit his position and make a play for you.

The other way a crush on a teacher can go wrong is if you start spreading rumours about you and the teacher. For a start, any teacher found to be having relations with a student, no matter if they are over 16 years old or not, could lose his job and his career. So think very carefully before you exaggerate a story, write him a love note, or make something up. A harmless action can have a devastating effect that can destroy someone else's life. The following story is what happened to a teacher when one of his students told everyone they were dating.

> It was my first job and I suppose I made quite a few mistakes when it came to dealing with this girl. I knew she had a crush on me because she wrote me love notes and told me face to face. She said she wanted to go out with me and that she loved me. I tried to be really calm and point out a teacher could never go out with a pupil. The next thing she did is went home and told her parents she was leaving school so she could go out with me.

They were furious and immediately came to the school and threatened legal action. The headmaster managed to persuade them nothing was going on, but he warned me to be careful. Then all hell broke loose. Her mother found a diary that had my name and address in and details about how we'd supposedly slept together. She was only 14 years old and I was suspended until further enquiries had been made by the police. My family stuck by me but my girlfriend couldn't handle it and left me. It was the worst time of my life. I felt everyone was pointing a finger at me and saying I was guilty.

The girl finally retracted everything because her best friend told the police she'd made it up, but I couldn't bear going back to work after that. I finally gave up teaching the year after.
Joe (27)

The truth about older men

If your crush is on an older man, going out with him isn't what you think it's going to be. If you're pining away hoping that this is the crush that will come true, then think again. An older man may give you the status and prestige you need but the price will be big. You'll grow up fast, whether you want to or not. A man will not be content to cuddle and kiss for hours, and some will even go so far as to apply sexual pressure to get what they want. On top of this, are you really going to be interested in his stories about work, and will he be interested in yours about school? The differences which seem so small when you've got a crush are actually huge when the relationship becomes real.

When I had a crush on Karl he was going out with a girl his age. I found out everything I could about him and then I started hanging around hoping he'd notice me. He finally did, and he'd always flirt with me. I think he was flattered that I liked him so much, and that I was so young. His girlfriend wasn't so pleased. Finally they split up and we ended up together, and that's when everything went wrong. I was 16 years old and he

CRUSHES ON OLDER MEN

said I was young and fresh compared to his ex who was 21. But I was still at school, and because of that he'd make fun of me and say I was a baby. I realize now that was just to get me to sleep with him. On top of that, he was such a flirt and whenever I complained he said I was being childish and immature. In the end he just got fed up with me and ditched me. It took me ages to get my self-confidence back.
Lucy (17)

As Lucy found out, the prestige of winning the attentions of an older guy isn't very long lasting. On top of that you have to ask yourself why he's interested in you. Is it because it looks good to his friends? Is it because he likes having his ego massaged by someone who admires him? Or is it something else all together? On the other hand, ask yourself, is it really the person who is attracting you or is it everything an older man can offer? Will you use him? Will he use you? And are some crushes worth making real?

I've always had crushes on older men; my mum says it's because my dad left when I was eight years old and I need security. I don't know if this is true but I do know that my crushes will always remain just crushes because I've seen too many of my friends hurt by older guys. The relationship is never equal and it never works out. It's all just a waste of time. Having a crush is hard enough to cope with without seeing it come true.
Kaye (14)

6
Crushes on Girls

So, you've got a crush on someone – you dream about them, you admire them, you want to be like them and you think you may even fancy them. But it's driving you crazy. Why? Simply because they're female, and so are you.

Am I normal?

The question you're probably asking yourself is, 'Am I normal if I fancy someone of the same sex?' and the answer is simply yes! Normality is a hard thing to define because it incorporates everything. The fact is, what's normal to one person isn't normal to another, but this doesn't mean it's wrong. For instance, if you live with your parents then that's normal to you, but to someone who just lives with one parent your situation isn't normal, but their's is.

When it comes to fancying people, the same rule applies. You may fancy sporty guys with long hair, while your friend prefers tall, short-haired men. This doesn't mean one of you is abnormal and one isn't. It just means that you prefer different things, which is great because imagine if we all fancied the same person. Of course, during our teenage years it isn't always easy to see this.

> I daren't tell anyone that I've got a crush on Donna. How can I, they'd think I was weird? My friends spend all their time talking about the boys they fancy. If I turned round and said I liked a girl, they'd run a mile.
> *Julie (14)*

As Julie points out, it's hard to stand up for what you believe in if it isn't what everyone else thinks. Apart from the internal

CRUSHES ON GIRLS

suffering of knowing you're different, you lay yourself open to all kinds of unwanted attention. From jokes behind your back to open bare-faced bullying, from people too stupid and ignorant to see that normal can and does mean anything.

> These girls found all these pictures of Julia Roberts in my desk and started calling me a lesbian. They didn't even give me a chance to explain that I just admired her, and it wasn't the kind of love they thought it was. But that didn't stop them from telling everyone I was gay and basically making me the butt of everyone's jokes. I was so upset, I eventually told my art teacher who made them leave me alone.
> *Sula (15)*

There are many reasons why you may have fallen for a female and only one of them might be that you're gay. During puberty, your emotions are bound to go haywire as you try to find out what makes you happy and what doesn't. It's very common for girls to have crushes on other girls, just as some find they have a lot of very strong short relationships with boys, while others never fall in love. It's also common for teenagers to experiment sexually with both boys and girls for a variety of different reasons.

> I fell in love with my best friend while we were away at boarding school. Now I know it was because I was terribly lonely there, but at the time I was so upset about it. I felt dirty and disgusting and thought I was doing something wrong.
> *Kim (27)*

> Miss Archer was my English teacher when I was 14 years old and she was so unlike any teacher I'd ever had. Young and funny, I just wanted to be like her. I'd always hang around her hoping she would look at me and be my best friend or something. I think now I was in love with her because when she announced she was getting married I was heart-broken.
> *Louise (29)*

CRUSHES ON GIRLS

Having a crush on the head girl when I was 13 years old was hard on me because I made it so obvious. All my friends used to tease me and say I was a lesbian. At the time I didn't know why I had a crush on her, but it lasted all the way through school. Now I realize it was because she was always so nice to me and no one else ever was.
Sian (25)

If you have had similar experiences to these girls, you can see that having a crush on someone of the same sex can and does happen for a variety of reasons. However, it may not be till years later that you realize why you actually did it. So, if you feel love for or fantasize about a girl, it doesn't mean you've decided on your sexuality, and it definitely doesn't mean you are abnormal. Remember, crushes are the first twinges of love and sexual feelings, and these feelings are natural, normal, and perfectly all right.

Three common same-sex crushes

Famous women

Madonna, Cindy Crawford, Julia Roberts – they all have the same things in common: success, beauty, and intelligence. They also happen to be three of the most desired women in the world. The stuff pure crushes are made of! If you have a crush on a famous woman, the chances are it has a lot more to do with fame and glamour than sexuality.

I adore Madonna. I have pictures of her all over my walls, I watch her on MTV and read everything about her. I suppose I have got a crush on her, but that's because I'd like to be her.
Fiona (14)

CRUSHES ON GIRLS

Sometimes I get confused about my feelings for this actress I like. She's really sexy and I worry that I may be abnormal liking her like I do.
Carol (15)

These girls are all trying to point out that their crushes are role models for them. It's important during puberty to have positive role models that give you some sort of idea of the kind of woman you want to be. This is why crushes on famous women are so common. Often we grow up in an area where there aren't many women we admire and find inspiring. Therefore, it's comforting to find a famous woman who has the kind of life or is the kind of person we'd like to be one day. It's healthy to feel this way and doesn't mean we're strange, odd, or weird in any way.

I started to really like Cindy Crawford when she admitted in a magazine that she was an ugly teenager who didn't have that many boyfriends. Also, so many people told her she couldn't be a supermodel and look at her now. It gives me hope that I won't always look like this.
Beth (16)

I can see that having a crush on a female singer really helped me. I used to collect everything on her and read anything I could get my hands on. My friends and parents thought I was strange but I loved her because not only was she attractive and famous but she came from a similar background to me. It made me realize I could be like her too if I tried. For a while, I thought I was in love with her, but when I got my first boyfriend I could see the difference in how I felt about her and how I felt about him. But I haven't forgotten my crush, because she was such a comfort to me when I didn't have anyone else to turn to.
Anna (27)

CRUSHES ON GIRLS

Best friends

Often as teenagers, the person we feel closest to is our best friend. In the space of a few short years she can become the person we most trust, admire and rely on. If this is true for you, then it's hardly surprising that the line between friendship and love can become blurred and confused. Soon the feelings that you took as friendship can take on new meaning and significance and the result can be a lost friendship and hurt feelings.

> Emma was my best friend for three years from 12 years old onwards. At first I liked her because she was so popular and I wasn't. As we became better friends, I started to idolize her and rely on her. Soon I started to get jealous of any guy she dated and became really tearful if she took their side against mine. I'd call her all the time and dream about her. In the end someone accused me of being a lesbian and I backed off from her and refused to see her. She didn't know why, and looking back now I can see that I really hurt her, but I didn't know how to deal with my feelings back then.
> *Yvette (18)*

If you've got a crush on your best friend, it's important to put it in perspective. Write a list of all the reasons why you think you love her as more than a friend. Then look at the list and see what you've written. Are her positive points all things you see as lacking in yourself? Are they the qualities you look for in a boyfriend and can't find? The answers to these questions will help you to decide your next step. If your crush on her is making things difficult for your friendship then you have to do one of two things or you may lose that friendship. Either talk to her and tell her how you feel, or talk to someone else. Often it can help to have an objective view of the situation before you approach your friend, and this way you can work out exactly what you're going to say. A telephone helpline (see end of chapter) is a good alternative to talking to someone face to face. Counsellors can help you to deal with your anxieties and will help you find the best way to deal with your crush.

Remember, before you do anything, what you say is likely to be a shock to your friend. Don't expect her to return your sentiments, because she probably won't. On the other hand, talking to her will help her to understand why you're behaving the way you are. If she really is a good friend, she'll want to work it out with you and won't just run off and refuse to be friends.

> I could never work out why Karen started acting so strangely towards me. One minute we were best friends and the next she wouldn't even talk to me. Years later she confessed she felt she was in love with me and couldn't handle it. I just wish she'd talked to me about it so we could have worked something out. Instead, I just thought I'd upset her or she'd gone off me. It was a very hard thing to deal with.
> *Lisa (18)*

Teachers

Like famous women, female teachers can easily become an object of someone's crush. After all, they are women that you see day in and day out. Women who teach you help you discover things about yourself that you've never noticed before.

> I come from a family where education isn't considered very important. I used to feel that way until I met my new English teacher. She is quite young and trendy and helped me see that I was good at something. My mum just laughs when I say I want to be a writer, but my teacher is always encouraging me. I think I'm in love with her, she is so lovely. My family tease me about her and I'm sure she knows, but I can't help feeling the way I do.
> *Billie (14)*

If you have a crush on one of your female teachers it's important not to let your feelings get out of control. By all means talk to her and tell her if you feel she can handle it. Lots of female teachers are well prepared for such things and can help you come to terms with your feelings. However, don't tell a lot of people how you feel unless you want your private feelings talked about behind your back and rumours to be thrown around. The fact is, there are bound to be a lot of immature people who won't be able to handle or understand your feelings.

Don't take your feelings for a teacher to be a sure sign you're gay. If you are, you'll know in time, but for the moment, don't be in such a rush to label yourself. Girls always have role models they feel they are in love with when they're growing up. These role models are important and significant parts of our lives. They can help us shape our future, decide what we want from relationships and guide us, but they are never anything more than that.

Having a crush on my art teacher, Mrs Derby, was an important part of my teenage years. For a long time I just wanted to be near her because I felt I was in love with her. Now I realize she filled a gap in my life. You see, my mother and I didn't get on, but Mrs Derby and I did. She really encouraged me to make the most of myself and I took this to be a sign she loved me. I think she did in a way, but not the way I hoped. Now I can see she is the reason I am a successful artist today. If she hadn't been there I don't know what would have happened to me.
Flynn (21)

Dealing with a same-sex crush

1 Make sure you tell someone how you feel.

Often girls feel guilty for idolizing another female, but it's no good locking all these feelings up in your head and hoping they'll go away. The fact is, they won't, and they'll only make you more and more miserable. Of course you have to be careful about who you tell, but your mum, an older sister, or best friend are usually a good bet. You'll be surprised at how liberating talking about your feelings can be.

> I used to be really worried about why I felt this way until I spoke to my mum. She was great, she told me about how she used to have a crush on her teacher and experienced the same things that I'm going through now.
> *Wendy (14)*

2 Telling the person you have a crush on isn't always a good idea.

For a start, they probably haven't got much of an inkling that you feel this way, and secondly, they may not know how to deal with it. Likewise, writing them a letter isn't always the best thing to do. Of course, if you know them well enough to feel they won't freak out, or you feel you'll go crazy if you don't tell them, then by all means do it. Yet, be prepared for the fact they may not be over the moon, and give them time to get used to the idea.

> I told Hannah how I felt and how I idolized her, thinking she would turn round and say she felt the same. She didn't. She wasn't nasty, but she said we couldn't have an equal friendship if I idolized her like that. She said I was her friend, and that's all I could ever be to her. I was devastated and never spoke to her again.
> *Gina (15)*

3 Write a list of all the reasons why you like this person.

This will help you see just why you feel so strongly for them and what you look for in an ideal partner. Ask yourself the following:

- What drew your attention to this person?
- What do you like about her?
- How does she make you feel?
- When did you realize it was love?

- What do you dislike about her?
- How do you think she'd react if you told her?
- Does this crush make you happy, sad, crazy? And why?

My mum said I had a crush on this girl because she was everything I wanted to be – popular, pretty, funny and clever. I thought about it and realized she was right. I didn't fancy her, I wanted to be her.
Naomi (14)

4 For a few girls, having a crush on another girl is the first sign that they could be gay.

Some girls do discover that they are gay at an early age, while for others it takes a number of years, and different partners, to make their decision. After all, discovering your sexuality is never easy. Some people have sexual encounters with people of the same sex and find they are not gay, and vice versa. But experimenting is all part of growing up and, whatever you feel or do, isn't a sign that you've decided on your sexuality. The most important thing is not to label yourself to suit other people. Keep an open mind about your sexuality and one day you'll know for sure whether you're gay/straight/bisexual or asexual. Being true to yourself is more important than what other people think of you.

Helplines

If you need someone confidential and sympathetic to talk to there are a number of organizations with helplines that you can call. Careline will help any teenagers worried or distressed about a problem. The Lesbian and Gay Switchboard has a 24-hour helpline for people worried about their sexuality. You will find their numbers listed at the end of this book in the Useful Addresses section.

7
Crushes That Come True

So far we've talked about crushes that don't have a chance of becoming real because of location, age, fame and sex. However, there is one type of crush that may well materialize into something concrete, and that's a crush on someone from your own peer group, someone you have a real chance of getting to know.

For most of us, the first step into a relationship is a tricky one. Unlike the movies, a single glance across a crowded room does not equal undying love and affection, and often long before a relationship even starts, an elaborate game of he-loves-me-he-loves-me-not begins. This is the crush stage, where you dream about him every night, discover his likes and dislikes, and do everything you can to get him to notice you.

The next stage is to decide whether or not you want your crush to become real. Your first answer may well be Yes, but really think about it. Have you built him up to be Superman in your imagination when he's only Clark Kent in real life? Before you do anything, ask yourself the following questions:

- Do you realize that the real man is very different from your dream man, that he'll have bad traits and habits like everyone else?
- Have you ever spoken more than two sentences to him?
- Are you attracted by more than his looks, job, popularity?
- Are you prepared for him to turn you down?
- Are you really sure you want a relationship?
- Are you sure he doesn't already have a girlfriend?
- Do you have anything in common?
- Do you think he may be attracted to you?

CRUSHES THAT COME TRUE

If you score more than five nos then really think about what you're doing and why.

Why your crush may work out

There are a number of reasons why your crush stands more of a chance of becoming real if your crush is someone you know locally. For a start, you have a common background, you live near each other, know the same people, are of relatively the same age. All these things form a solid base for a relationship to start from. And though it doesn't mean your crush will fall at your feet and swear undying love, it does mean the cards are stacked more in your favour than if you had a crush on a pop star.

The following are stories from girls whose crushes became real, for better or for worse.

Lee was my brother's best friend and I had fancied him for ages. I used to keep a picture of him in my diary and went about trying to be as near to him as possible. I'd had crushes in the past and this one went along the same path. One minute I was happy, the next sad. I used to feel over the moon if I knew he was coming round and dreadful when he went home. One night my sister asked me why I was doing this to myself. She said my crush wasn't like a crush on a pop star who was out of reach and I could do something about it if I wanted to. I'd never thought about it that way; I'd been so used to putting people out of reach on pedestals that I'd forgotten that he was a real person. Realizing this helped me to talk to him and a few months later we ended up going out.
Yoko (17)

Sometimes, having a crush on someone near is harder than on someone who is out of reach. Mainly because you've got less excuses why it can't come true and this makes it scarier because it might actually happen. I had a crush on this boy called Mark, till I heard that he liked me back and that put me

off. Not because I thought he was horrible, but because I wasn't ready for a relationship. I was too scared of disappointment and heart-break if he didn't live up to my image of him.
Mary (16)

Having a relationship with someone you used to have a crush on is hard because, whenever things go bad, you find yourself comparing him to your ideal image. It's really unfair because no one could live up to that even if they wanted to. Also, it's not accepting them for what they are, and that isn't what a relationship is all about. In my experience, it's almost as if your boyfriend and your crush are two different people and you're trying to make them one.
Elaine (17)

Having a crush on my boyfriend Will for two months before we went out really helped. It was almost as if I got a preview of what it was going to be like before we started. It helped me to deal with problems that arose later on, and finding out about him from his friends gave me a chance to decide whether we had anything in common or not. Also, he was flattered when he heard how much I liked him and that kind of got us together.
Dawn (16)

Why you should go for it

At college I had a friend who had a mad and desperate crush on our flatmate's best friend. She miserably watched him from afar, spoke about him all the time, collected as much info as she could on him, went to places she knew he'd be at, and even sent him an anonymous Valentine's card. She thought she was making her feelings very obvious, but at the same time she never spoke to him, always looked down when he looked at her, and convinced herself he was just too handsome for her. The result was that nothing ever happened and she stayed miserable. Two years

CRUSHES THAT COME TRUE

later, I bumped into him on the street and he confessed that he used to fancy her but knew she never liked him. When I told her she was dumbstruck because she thought she'd made her feelings clear to him. Now she considers the whole episode a wasted opportunity and kicks herself for not having the courage to go after what she wanted.

The moral of this story is that it is better to go after what you want, and fail, than never go after it at all. It's also better to find out if you stand a chance than sit about miserable and unhappy because all you've got is a dream to hold onto. The fact is, many girls are guilty of doing this in the name of love. We hide behind a thousand obstacles, saying if only . . . this happened, or this, or this. Many of us do nothing because we're afraid of rejection, and would rather live in hope than with no hope at all.

> I can't ask him out, I'm too scared and too afraid he'll laugh. I just hope he'll get the hint I like him or ask me out instead. I talk about him all the time and I couldn't bear it if he went out with someone else, but I just can't tell him I like him.
> *Fiona (16)*

Often, we spend so much time thinking about the person we like, talking about him to our friends, dreaming of him, and accidentally bumping into him, that we assume we're making our intentions very obvious when we're not.

> I'd had a crush on Steve for two years and I assumed he knew all about it. After all it had been on my mind for all that time and my friends knew all about it because we hung around him and his friends all the time. But when we started going out he said he'd known nothing about it. He hadn't even noticed I liked him.
> *Kelly (16)*

The real reason most people don't go after the person they

want is fear of rejection. Everyone hates it, dreads it, and it's the one thing that stops most people from getting what they want. If you recognize it as the reason for your crushes, then fine. In time you'll realize that rejection is not as scary as you may think, and you can and will confront it.

However, if you're a person who would love a boyfriend but finds no one 'wonderful, exciting or glamorous' ever comes your way, or that boyfriends never live up to your high expectations, then it's time for a rethink. Perhaps you're mixing up your fantasy world with the real world. Okay, that boy who asked you out isn't the man you've been dreaming of, but he may be nice if you give him a chance. Anyway, he has one advantage over your crush; he's here in the flesh. So, try talking to him and you may be surprised at how interesting a 'normal' person can be.

I always had this idea that the man I'd fall in love with would be like one of my crushes. He'd have movie-star looks, talent and money. We'd go off to foreign exotic places and I'd never have to do mundane things like cook and work. This attitude meant that I was probably the only girl in my class that never had a date till she was 20 years old. The man I'm in love with now is nothing like the man I thought I would end up with, but strangely enough it doesn't matter. If you really love someone all those other things don't matter.
Tanya (23)

The pros and cons of approaching your crush

So you've made the decision to talk to the man you've had a crush on for all this time. The problem is how do you do it? Well, it may not feel easy but it is simple – be yourself. Remember, if he doesn't like you for you, then he'd make a useless boyfriend, and you'd be better off without him. Also, bear in mind that you may not actually like the real person. The danger of crushes is that it's easier to fall in love with someone in your mind, because you can project all the nice qualities of the world onto them, like generosity, kindness, humour, etc. The reality will always be different because he's bound to be a normal human being with normal vices, like you and me.

> For the three months I had a crush on Kevin I always assumed he was a nice person because he was always making people laugh and was very, very funny. When I started hanging around with him, I saw the reality was he made fun of people weaker than himself and didn't like it if someone made him the butt of their jokes. It was such a disappointment.
> *Louise (16)*

Moulding yourself to be the person you think he'd like is dangerous as well. Fran had a crush on her school sports captain.

> I loathed sport but because I knew Dan was a major sports fan I pretended to be interested as well. I read up on everything I could find, and then volunteered to help out on the teams. I was always the one who turned up in the pouring rain to support his team. I was the one who helped carry the equipment. When we started going out, I had to watch endless hours of sport when I'd much rather have been at the cinema with my friends. In the end I hated him and sport and it wasn't even his fault.
> *Fran (15)*

Being interested in things they like is part of being a couple, but pretending to like something you don't is a lie and bound to end in disaster. So, once you've decided to be yourself, the next few steps are easier.

1 Go and talk to him.
Yes, I know this sounds like a fate worse than death, but it isn't.

CRUSHES THAT COME TRUE

It's only through talking that you're going to discover the real man and decide whether or not you really like him.

> I was worried about going to talk to him because everyone says there's no way a person can live up to a crush, but they're wrong. Julian was even nicer when I got to know him, and now I wish I hadn't wasted three months dreaming about him instead of talking to him.
> *Maggie (16)*

2 Look at him while you speak.

Don't look at your shoes, or his left ear, and listen to what he's saying instead of pondering on all those imaginary conversations you've had in your head, or the time you kissed him for three hours in your mind. These things will only distract, embarrass and freak you out.

> I had this crush on my parents' friends' eldest son, and one day he came over to dinner with his parents and I had to sit opposite him. It was terrible. I couldn't even look at him let alone talk to him, because all I kept thinking was the time I dreamt we'd had sex together. I didn't eat anything and refused to answer anyone's questions. I came across as a complete idiot.
> *Justine (17)*

3 Don't blurt out how much you know about him straight away.

It will make him think either the FBI's been investigating him or you're someone straight out of *Fatal Attraction*.

> I remember this boy coming up to me and asking me out. He said he'd fancied me for ages and I was flattered until he started dropping in all these things about me. Like where I hung out, what my brothers were called, who my friends were. I was so scared I thought he was some kind of psycho.
> *Nina (16)*

CRUSHES THAT COME TRUE

4 If your mind goes blank then just ask him questions about himself.

Most people love to talk about themselves and it takes the emphasis off you having to do all the chatting.

> I used to lie awake at night and think I must talk to him, I must talk to him. Then I'd worry about what to say, what he'd think of me, and then I'd be depressed because I knew I could never actually approach him. Then one day we got chatting because he came up and asked if he could borrow my history book.
> *Cathy (15)*

5 If it all goes wrong and he's not interested, then go and cry on a friend's shoulder and put it down to experience.

At least now you know where you stand and you can stop wasting your time on him and find someone even better.

> I was miserable when I had a crush on him because it was so frustrating and miserable when I asked him out and he said no. But now I feel better because I know there's no chance we'll get together, so I've gone off him. It's quite a relief really.
> *Julie (16)*

6 If he isn't too communicative don't be put off.

Boys have really bad bouts of shyness like us girls; they get intimidated and scared too. Remember, you've had weeks of time to analyze what's going to happen and why, while he's just been dumped in the deep end.

> My friends and I had thought of everything he might say and do when I went up to him, and I thought we had covered everything, but we hadn't. I said 'hello' and he just looked at me and nodded. At first I thought, 'Oh no, he hates me. He won't talk to me. I've been a fool.' Then I realized it wasn't

any of those things. It was just that he didn't know what to say next.
Sunitra(15)

7 Don't read too much into what he says.

Again, it's easy when you like someone to take something they say and blow it out of proportion. Remember, no matter how long you've had a crush on him, you don't really know him yet. Take things slow and easy.

> I just took too much for granted when it came to Keith. I spent so much time dreaming about him, and how we'd get together, that when he finally talked to me I took it as a sign of love and it scared him off.
> *Michelle (17)*

8 If you find you've been flirting with him for weeks and weeks and still he shows no sign of asking you out, then try to be realistic.

Often we pick guys who are out of reach or unsuitable because we don't really feel ready for a relationship.

> Danny was the first boy I ever fell for. I put him on a pedestal because I thought he was wonderful, talented, and everything I wanted. You see, I had had a crush on him for a year and when we started going out I was so happy. But it wasn't long before he found he couldn't cope with my image of him. He left me, saying I was in love with a dream not with the real him, and my impossible standards were too hard to live up to.
> *Sara (19)*

8
When a Crush Becomes an Obsession

At the bottom line crushes are supposed to be fun and enjoyable. As we've shown earlier in the book, crushes are a safe way of falling in love. They protect you from the down side of relationships, and bolster your confidence for the positive side. Apart from the odd negative moment when you feel like the whole world is working against you, crushes are on the whole a fulfilling experience.

However, they can quickly turn into a living nightmare if you start to believe that you are genuinely in love with the other person and are being cheated out of a life with them. For some girls, the frustration then becomes unbearable, and a crush turns into an obsession.

> When I was 15 years old I had a crush on Tim who lived next door to me. It was good fun in the beginning fancying him. I laughed about it with my friends and we made up scenarios of how I'd get together with him and what we'd do on our dates. Even what we'd call our children. Then I started thinking about him so much that I got really frustrated about the whole thing. I started to imagine if his girlfriend wasn't around Tim would ask me out and we'd be together. I became obsessed with the idea, and determined to split them up. It got to the point where my friends would have nothing to do with me because I spent all my time following Tim and slagging off his girlfriend. Then, when he'd tell me to get lost, I'd cry my eyes out for hours. Eventually my school work went down hill and I lost loads of weight. Finally, Tim complained to my mum and she took me to see a counsellor. She was really nice and over a couple of months helped me to see how distorted my view of

WHEN A CRUSH BECOMES AN OBSESSION

my relationship with Tim had become. It's only when I realized that I was holding onto something that didn't really exist that I finally let go of my idea of him.
Jackie (19)

I wouldn't call what I have a crush as I am really in love with him. You see, I've read everything there is on him and I just know we're made for each other. We have the same dislikes and likes and I'm very like his description of his ideal girl. I know where he lives and I go and hang outside his place nearly every day and write him letters about how I feel. He's got this model girlfriend at the moment but I know he'll soon get sick of her because she's just using him because he's famous. One day we'll end up going out, it just hasn't happened yet because our paths haven't crossed.
Janie (14)

If my teacher didn't have a girlfriend I know he'd go out with me. I can tell by the way he smiles at me and talks to me. Whenever I see him it's like there's this chemical reaction between us. So what if he's five years older than me and they've been going out for six years, I know he secretly fancies me.
Tricia (15)

These girls are examples of crushes that have become obsessions. They are unable to face up to the reality that they are not really having a relationship with the object of their desires. In their minds their love is only being thwarted by some specific event, person, a situation that is out of their control and out of the control of their prospective 'boyfriend'. Like most people who find their crush is becoming an obsession, they live in if only . . . land. If only . . . he noticed me . . . If only he didn't have a girlfriend, etc. They ignore the real reasons why their crush won't become real, so their fantasies look as if they could come true. Soon, they start to live their life as if they are having a real relationship with their crush, and that's when all the problems associated with crushes become magnified and harder to bear.

How to know if your crush has become an obsession

- Are you unable to work, sleep, and eat properly?
- Do you spend more time thinking about him than anything else?
- Do you have a lack of interest in life and other people?
- Do you constantly play over scenarios in your mind about him?
- Do you spend your time hanging around places you know he goes to?
- Does the frustration of not being with him drive you to tears every day?
- Can you see no future without him?
- Would you feel like your life was ruined for ever if he got married tomorrow?
- Do you feel physically ill with anxiety when you think of him?
- Do you believe you could never be happy without him?

If you scored more than three yeses then your crush is well on the way to becoming an obsession and it's time to do something positive. You'd be wise to take a deep breath and put your feelings into perspective.

Losing your heart and then giving up your life for someone who is either unavailable or out of reach is an invitation to unhappiness and despair. The hard fact is, even if they do know you're alive, they won't have planned your future together in the immense detail you have. And if by some chance you do get together, the relationship is almost certain to fail because no relationship could live up to the perfect one in your head.

Dan and I had been best friends all through college and over that time I really fell for him even though he had a long-

WHEN A CRUSH BECOMES AN OBSESSION

standing girlfriend at home. In my imagination, he and I had this perfect relationship where we never argued and were always happy. Over time I forgot it was all in my head and took everything he did to be a sign of love for me. In our last term together, my feelings went out of control. When we went out I'd pretend we were dating and tell my friends what had happened, blowing small things out of proportion, so they'd think he really liked me and encourage me. I became so convinced we were in love that I secretly found a flat for us to live in together when we finished college. The one thing that worried me was he still hadn't broken up with his girlfriend. So on our last day at college I rang her up and told her what was going on. The next thing I knew, Dan came round and started screaming at me, demanding to know what was going on. I told him I knew we were meant to be together and then told him about the flat. He didn't say anything. He just looked at me like I was mad and left. I never saw him again.
Sarah (23)

If only Sarah had told Dan what was going on in her mind then he could have told her he wasn't interested. Then, even though she would have been hurt, she could have put her feelings into perspective and saved herself a lot of pain. Instead, she started reading messages in the smallest things Dan did, imagining it to be a secret code between them. At the same time, she encouraged her friends to pep her up by blowing these incidents out of proportion. With her friends on her side she 'proved' to herself that she wasn't imagining everything and that Dan's love for her was real. By the time she had done all this, she'd crossed the line between fact and fiction and no longer knew what was real and what wasn't. The result was a lost friendship, a broken heart, despair, and regret.

Don't let this happen to you. Be realistic about what you're doing and what you have. If you can keep your feelings and thoughts just in dream land, then fine, but if you find it creeping into your daily life, then you must do something before it gets out of control.

What to do

Talk to someone

Crushes become distorted when you play things over and over in your mind and then let the frustration drive you crazy. If you find this happening then you must talk to someone. Often an objective outsider, like a counsellor, can offer the most help. This is because you won't be afraid to tell him or her the whole truth as everything you say will be completely confidential. Talking about your worries, anxieties, and general feelings can be like someone lifting a weight off your shoulders. The following organizations can and will offer you sympathetic help: Childline, Youth Access, the Samaritans, RELATE (National Marriage Guidance Council). Information about these organizations, plus their addresses and phone numbers, is at the back of this book.

> I found talking to my mother really helped. One night she came in and asked me why I never went out with my friends any more and just sat about listening to my records. She asked me if I was unhappy, and it all just came pouring out. I ended up telling her everything. About how frustrated and miserable I was. About how I followed this guy about all day in the hope he'd notice me. About the letters I'd written and he'd never replied to, and the way I couldn't concentrate on anything besides him. She just listened, and when I was finished she said I mustn't spend so much time on my own because it would just make me think about him even more. From then on, she always made sure I went out with my friends or came and did something with her. It really helped to make me think about other things beside him.
> *Jo (15)*

Be practical

Being practical about who you fall for may not be exciting or romantic, but it will make you heaps happier in the long run. Of course, it's not easy. It's hard to stop dreaming about a movie star when the scenery around you isn't exactly glamorous. But learning to give those boys nearer to you a chance is a start. Remember, you're just dating them, not planning to spend your whole lives with them, and it doesn't mean you have to stop having your own private fantasies.

I have always had crushes on famous men and my last one lasted a year. I thought I'd always feel like this and could never imagine dreaming about an ordinary boy this way until I met Craig. He worked part time in this record store I used to hang out in because I knew this singer always went there. He wasn't anything special but he was funny and made me laugh about my obsession on this singer. Over time I realized I was going to the shop not to see the singer but to see him. Now we're going out and I'm very happy. It's much nicer to have someone ordinary in the flesh than someone glamorous in your head.
Yvette (17)

Is it his life-style you're attracted to? Ask yourself if it really is your dream man or his life-style you yearn for. Sometimes, you'll find it's the promise of what he's got to offer that lures you to him.

I used to work part time as a waitress in this really posh restaurant and every night this guy would come in. He was only slightly older than me but he obviously had money: he was well dressed, had a sports car, and some kind of flash advertising career. I really liked him and would always serve him and he'd tease me and say he was in love with me. I became so obsessed that on my days off I'd wait outside the restaurant just to catch a glimpse of him. After months and months of this, he actually asked me out, but it was a disaster. He was so boring and we had nothing in common. It was then I realized it was his life I was obsessed with not him.
Veronica (19)

WHEN A CRUSH BECOMES AN OBSESSION

If, like Veronica, you are obsessed with a life-style your crush represents, be it fame or fortune, then put all your efforts into that. At the end of the day, being obsessed with a dream that is about you is far healthier than putting all your efforts into getting a man who's a key to that life-style.

Don't look for clues

When we fall in love with someone it's easy to search for signs from them that they are interested in us: signs like shy smiles, words and hearsay. However, it's also easy to take these things out of context and read more into them. Learning to be careful about the assumptions you make will protect you from reading a situation wrongly.

> Over time I've learned not to read too much into things. In the past, I've been guilty of loving someone from afar then letting myself believe that they love me back. One guy I had a crush on wrote me a note about some college work and put 'love Mark' on it, and I took that as a sign. Another time, I persuaded myself this teacher liked me because he stopped to talk to me on the street. At the end of the day, I've learnt the hard way, through embarrassment and humiliation, that you shouldn't take anything for granted unless someone says it outright.
> *Haley (18)*

So, if your dreams and secret love affairs are driving you crazy and making you do crazy things, then practise turning off those dreams. This is the only way you're going to see your 'real' life clearly. Remember, the point of love is to have someone you can really rely on, joke with, cry on, and be friends with. And let's face it, at the end of the day, dream men don't equal any of those things.

Practise getting your life in order

This means maintaining a 'normal' life as much as you can. Make sure you eat three healthy meals a day even if you really can't bear to. Eating healthily is the key to a healthy mind. If you starve your body of its nutrients and of food, you are going to feel more depressed, lethargic, and generally unhappy.

Don't neglect your schoolwork. Working on getting the man you love is no consolation for failing all your exams. No one likes working for exams, and day-dreaming is a far nicer alternative, but this won't get you anywhere in the world. Set aside the necessary time for your work, and, apart from helping you to pass your exams, it will help train your mind to stop thinking about your dream man.

Getting eight hours of sleep isn't always easy when all you've got on your mind is the object of your affections. It's easy to lie awake and worry yourself into insomnia because this is the one time of the day when you have no other distractions and no way of telling someone how miserable you are. If this sounds like you, there is an easy way to get rid of your worries. Try this kind of personal therapy. The next time you're lying awake fretting all night, get up and get a piece of paper. Then write down exactly how you feel (you can write it as a letter to him, if you prefer), your worries, your hopes, your fears, why you love him, why you're not with him, in fact anything that's on your mind. Don't bother reading it after you're finished, as it will make you feel self-conscious. Just tear it up, and throw it away. You'll be surprised to see how relieved you feel and how easy it will be to sleep.

Eight tips on how to stop getting obsessed

1 Don't spend hours alone thinking about him. It's easy to drift off in a fantasy when you are by yourself listening to soppy records. But this will make you unhappy and obsessive in the long run.
2 Don't cut yourself off from your friends. Make sure you still go

WHEN A CRUSH BECOMES AN OBSESSION

out, even if you don't want to. Friends are very important and if you ignore them they'll soon start ignoring you back.

3 Talk about it to someone sensible when you're down. It's easy to rush off to see another friend who's got a crush when you're down, but ask yourself, is she really going to give you some sound, down-to-earth advice? Speak to someone who may not tell you what you want to hear but will be sympathetic.

4 Don't do anything you know is considered obsessive. This means don't follow him about and blow his actions out of proportion.

5 Don't skip from him saying 'hello' to suddenly seeing yourself married with five kids. Take everything step by step, and as slowly as possible. This way you won't fool yourself into thinking something has happened when it hasn't.

6 Don't turn down other dates. Hard one this one, especially if you don't fancy anyone but him. However, it's the best way to work out the difference between a real affair and one in your mind.

7 Be honest (even if it's painful) and write down all the things wrong with your potential relationship. Things like: he has a girlfriend, he's famous, he lives in America, he's married, he's 15 years older than you, he doesn't know you're alive. Stick them on your wall as a reminder to you that your relationship isn't real.

8 Get your friends to give you reality checks to stop you getting carried away. Make them pull you down to earth even if you don't appreciate it. This way you won't get carried away on a day-dream.

9
Boys With Crushes

Reading this book, it's easy to think girls are the only ones who ever get crushes. The truth is, crushes happen to everyone, male or female, they don't discriminate. However, the pain of having a crush when you're male is often nightmarish because it's so much more unacceptable to everyone around you. After all, most boys view them as 'girly', 'soft', 'weak willed', and 'pathetic'.

> I think it's more acceptable for a girl to have a crush. People think you're a wimp or strange if you say you love someone like a model or actress.
> *Jim (17)*

> It's okay to say things like she's got nice legs, I fancy a bit of her. Or I wouldn't mind one night with that actress, but if I said I'd love to have a relationship with her because I read she's really nice and we'd get on, my friends would die laughing. So I have to keep all my day-dreams to myself.
> *Steve (16)*

> It is easier for girls, because they can talk to their mates about how they feel. I had a crush on this girl in a band and went along with my sister to see them play. But I was so embarrassed when I got there because I was one of the only guys around. Everyone else was female and there because they had a crush on the singer. I felt like everyone was looking at me.
> *Raj (15)*

Having a crush is an embarrassment for most boys. Many say it makes them feel pathetic because it proves to the world they can't get a 'real' girlfriend and, therefore, have to dream one up in their head. Unlike girls, they don't recognize the benefits of such a 'safe' relationship. This is why most boys would rather keep their crushes and day-dreams to themselves than tell their best mate about them. No matter if the crush makes them wildly happy, or interminably sad, they prefer to keep their feelings locked up. Unlike girls, they feel bad about revelling in their crushes and any time they do take out to day-dream is considered somewhat ridiculous.

> Having a crush on Annette was a bizarre experience. It really threw me. I felt stupid all the time and whenever I saw her I'd get totally speechless and mumble something incoherent. But my friends thought it was really funny and would really take the mickey out of me. It was actually a very upsetting time, because I felt very cut off from everyone. Eventually I met a girl on holiday and started going out with her. When I came back my crush had thankfully disappeared.
> *Joe (18)*

> When I fancied Anna I couldn't tell anyone. She was the most popular girl in school, good at sports and pretty, while I was shy and not at all sporty. I mentioned it to my friend once and he said 'Who doesn't fancy her?' Then I felt really crushed because it made me feel like I didn't have a chance at all. After that I felt miserable whenever I thought about her.
> *Eric (16)*

> I get crushes all the time but I'd never tell my friends because they just wouldn't understand. Can you imagine me saying I love this girl I don't even know? They'd think I was crazy. I know lots of girls get crushes but then that's just part of being one of the gang for them.
> *Lloyd (15)*

BOYS WITH CRUSHES

Learning to be open

Unlike girls, boys' friends are not towers of strength. They can be relied upon to be there for a laugh, a night out, and other such social events, but most don't want to be there when you're down.

> I can't tell you how difficult it is to be honest with my mates. I can't tell them my feelings because I know most of them wouldn't be able to handle it. This makes having a crush extremely hard and lonely.
> *Pete (16)*

Unfortunately, the best way to deal with a crush is to be open and frank about it. If you can't be open with the people closest to you, then coping is going to be very tough going. Learning to discuss problems with your friends may seem like the hardest thing in the world, but all it takes is a bit of courage, honesty, and will-power. And who knows, perhaps all your friends are waiting for is an excuse to open up and talk for themselves.

> One day I got so unhappy about how I felt that I had to talk about it. When I told my two best friends how I felt, they went really quiet and I thought, 'Oh no!' Then one of them said 'God, I know how you feel. I liked this girl and never told anyone', and then the other joined in as well. It made me realize that we were all dying to talk but were too worried about what everyone else thought of us.
> *Paul (16)*

Tips on how to talk about your crush

1 Don't beat around the bush. Just bring up the subject of unrequited love and see how your friends react.
2 If you can't voice your worries and fears in the first person, then make up a fictitious friend who has a crush on someone and doesn't know what to do. Then see what they say. You can always come clean later.

3 Don't tell them anything you don't feel comfortable about. Talking about your crush doesn't mean telling them everything you have dreamt about.
4 Ask your mum, sisters, female friends how they talk about delicate subjects with their friends.
5 Realize that crushes are perfectly natural and normal, and that everyone gets them. They're nothing to be ashamed of, so don't put yourself down.
6 Be careful who you talk to. Not everyone is perfect to confide in. So don't pick the friend who likes to have a joke at everyone else's expense or you'll end up being the butt of his jokes the next time you're out.

How to handle your crush

I always used to tease my sister about her crushes, so I guess it was my payback when I got one, on one of her friends. This girl was really pretty and popular at school, and I just didn't know how to approach her. Every time she came round I'd either ignore her or make some kind of stupid comment. It drove me mad because I knew I was making a fool of myself, but at the same time I couldn't stop thinking about her. Then I heard she was going out with this older guy and I was really heart-broken. The whole thing was so frustrating because I knew logically I didn't have anything to feel hurt about. But I really felt like I'd been rejected, and the feeling lasted for ages because I couldn't turn to anyone for sympathy.
Daniel (18)

So, now you know how to talk to your friends about your crush, what can you do about making the actual crush more bearable? If you're not sure if it's causing you any worries, ask yourself, is it driving you mad? Making you sad? Putting you off other girls. Making you feel bad about yourself and/or making you lose friends? Well, if it's doing any of these things, don't give up, there are ways you can learn to handle what's happening to you.

BOYS WITH CRUSHES

1 Try to talk to her.

Scary thought, but if she's someone you know, like a girl in your school, someone at work, or a friend's friend, then talking to her is the best way to get her to notice you. Talking to the person you have a crush on is also a good way to take them out of the dream realm and into the real world. Once you realize they talk about the same things as you do, you can start to let them down off their pedestal.

If you're really stuck for something to say, then always remember two rules: listen and ask questions. Bear in mind that talking doesn't mean having to confess exactly how you feel about her. However, if you are intent on telling her how you feel, be subtle about it. Blurting out that you've loved her from afar for five months may flatter her at first, but when you start telling her everything you know about her, she'll start to worry you're some kind of odd person and run a mile.

> Lola is a girl who worked part time with me. I fancied her the minute I saw her but, because I was so intimidated by her looks, I couldn't speak to her. She'd say something to me and my voice would just die in my throat. Finally, she just gave up and I heard her telling someone she thought I was really unfriendly. I kept thinking, if only you knew how I really felt.
> *Karl (16)*

2 Going for it.

In previous chapters, we've talked about why you should go for your crush if it's someone you know. Obviously, if your crush is on a pop star, your chances of it becoming real are somewhat limited. However, if you do know the person then you need to ask yourself, what have you got to lose by asking them out? Of course, if they are dating someone else, are a teacher, or someone much older, you're just asking for trouble. Try and gauge the situation and work out whether or not you really stand a good chance.

BOYS WITH CRUSHES

I had a crush on my present girlfriend for a year before we started going out. During that year I was mostly unhappy because I used to see her every day and could never say anything. Then I gradually got to know her, and then it was easier to ask her out. Now she tells me she had a crush on me for that time too, and if I had never asked her out she would never have believed I felt the same.
Tony (17)

3 Don't hide amongst your friends.

It's no good sitting about and thinking she'll never notice you, if you are always out with a crowd of friends. Think about how you'd feel if the situation were reversed. Try to rationalize why you feel like hiding from her sight amongst your friends. Is it because you're afraid she'll see you and won't like you back? Or because you'll show yourself up in some way? Or even that she'll be with someone and you'll feel crushed? The basis of all these feelings is a fear of rejection. Everyone hates it and everyone is scared of it, but don't let it stop you from making something you dream about real.

Tim and I are good friends now and it still surprises me when he reminds me he had a crush on me for a year and a half. I knew him all that time and I had no idea. Then again, I always say, how would I have known? He spent all his time back then with his five mates. All they ever used to do was hang out together, make crude jokes, and do stupid things. I would have had to have been a mind reader to know what he was thinking.
Jeanette (18)

5 It's okay to keep your crush as a crush.

So far we've talked about ways to make your crush aware of you, in case you want to make it real. However, it's important to add that it's also okay to keep your crush just as a crush and there's nothing wrong with that. The whole point of crushes is that they are a safe and unscary way of falling in love. And, often, most people would rather die that confront the object of their desires. This doesn't make them weak or silly, it just means they are being honest about what they're doing and why.

> The thought of facing her and telling her how I feel scares me to death. Once my friend tried to set me up with her and I nearly passed out. There's just no way I could ever handle having something with her. Not after all this time.
> *Nick (15)*

> A lot of my friends have got this crush on this model. She's really beautiful and seems quite funny. I guess most of us know we'd never really go out with anyone like that but that's part of the fun. Having a crush is not serious, in the way most girls take it, we just fantazise about her, that's all.
> *Will (17)*

6 *Don't ponder on her all day long.*

It's hard, when you've only got one thing that makes you happy, to stop thinking about it all the time. After all, what's the point in dealing with the everyday boring parts of life, when you can happily lay back and dream about her. The fact is, though day-dreaming is very pleasant and enjoyable, it is also a negative experience when you overdo it. It makes everyday life seem useless and everyday people who pass through your life dull.

> I never went out with anyone for three years because of this crush I had. I used to think about her so much that the women I actually met were boring by comparison. To be honest, I don't know if even she could have lived up to my day-dreams. That's the problem with crushes. They cloud your vision and make you forget what's real and what isn't.
> *Mark (19)*

If you think you may be guilty of this, concentrate on controlling how long you think about your crush. Pull yourself back into the present whenever you think you may be overdoing it and set aside times of the day when you can do it and when you can't. Also, give those other girls a chance. They may not be the superwoman of your dreams but at least they are real.

7 *Don't take rejection as a sign you're useless.*

There's a point in all crushes where you start to feel as if you've been rejected. It may come when you hear she prefers men that are six feet tall and muscley when you know you're five feet six with no pecs. Or, perhaps you tried to talk to her and it didn't work out. Or maybe you heard on the TV that she was madly in love with someone else and was going to marry him. This is the time when everything comes tumbling down, all the dreams you had for each other, and all the plans. This is also the time when you're likely to feel at your most vulnerable and sad.

> I heard she got married to some actor and I was devastated. I knew she was out of my reach, but in the back of my mind I kind of hoped one day I'd get to meet her and she'd fall for me. I don't care what anyone says, everyone who has a crush thinks this way. If you didn't consider that they might just come true one day, you wouldn't bother going through them.
> *Jimmy (16)*

If this has happened to you, don't give up. Breaking up with your crush is part of having a crush. After all, crushes are a preparation for the trials and tribulations of a real relationship. Remember rejection doesn't mean you're not good enough, worthy enough, or useless. It simply means the person you have fallen for has picked someone else. At the end of the day, whether you agree or not, it's better to know where you stand, so that you can move on, than keep on loving someone who has nothing to offer you.

BOYS WITH CRUSHES

8 You will grow out of it.
At some point, either your crush will become something concrete or else it will fade away. Even if you don't believe this now, the fact is all crushes eventually fade away to make room for something real. It's no good clinging on for dear life and shouting, 'I refuse to give up on this one', because when the flame's gone it's gone and there's nothing you can do about it.

> It was weird, I never expected my crush to just disappear, I thought I was going to feel like this for ever. At first I was upset because I liked the feeling of being in love. Now I feel quite relieved because I've started to see if I can find someone real to go out with me.
> *Paul (17)*

If a boy has a crush on you

You've just discovered that there's a boy who has a mad and passionate crush on you. What do you do? Well, the main rule here is always to be nice. Treat him the way you'd expect to be treated if the situation was reversed. If you like him, then your problems are solved. However, if you don't, don't reject him nastily. Boys are every bit as under-confident (despite their bravado) as you and I. They are petrified of rejection and scared of falling in love, and most (like us) need to be treated with kid gloves.

> I fancied Anna for ages and dreamt about her every day. I really wanted to go out with her because she seemed so nice. But when I asked her out she just laughed in my face and said 'You must be joking.' I was heart-broken.
> *Eric (16)*

So, he's got a crush on you. What do you do next?

BOYS WITH CRUSHES

1 *Don't encourage him if you don't fancy him.* When you know a boy fancies you then it can be very tempting to flirt with him because you know he'll give you attention. This is fine for you because you can then walk away with a boost to your confidence, while he's left thinking 'she does like me after all'.
2 *Don't be flattered into falling for him.* It's easy when you hear someone facies you to fancy them back. Not because you like them, but because it's comforting to think someone has been thinking of you. Relationships that start like this can often end in disaster as you won't have thought about what you're doing.
3 *Remember, if you say yes to him, a crush is hard to live up to.* Most boys with crushes are very guilty of putting their crushes on pedestals. This means, you'll always have an awful lot to live up to when you go out with them. It's hard to compete with a dream girl, especially if she looks just like you, but doesn't shout, get annoyed, or have bad habits. The best way to handle this is to talk about it with your boyfriend before it gets out of hand.
4 *If you know he has a crush on you and you like him back then go for it.* He may never work up the courage to ask you out and if you don't ask him then you may lose out on a good opportunity.
5 *If his crush freaks you out, because he keeps ringing, following you about, writing you letters or hanging about then you must tell someone what's going on.* Go by your instincts. If you feel at all threatened by his behaviour, or what he says, then make sure you get someone to put a stop to what he's doing. Parents, older siblings, friends, and teachers are good bets.

10

Crushes On Boys

Am I Gay?

This is probably one of the most common refrains to go through a teenage boy's or girl's mind. Why? Well, during adolescence our bodies start to mature sexually and this is when we start to become aware of other people as sexual objects. However, for boys more than girls, it is a time of great upset and confusion. This is because many boys find that the direction of their sexuality goes haywire and suddenly they start fantasizing about men, when supposedly all they're meant to fancy are women.

For many, the sexual guilt from these fantasies is completely overwhelming and terrifying. Mixed with homophobia, machismo, the pressure to have sex and get a girlfriend, it's little wonder that most boys have a tough time of it and end up confused, distraught and miserable.

> Sometimes, I don't know whether I'm coming or going. My mum's always going on about having a girlfriend. My Dad wants me to become a rugby player, and my friends want to know if I've 'done it' yet. The truth is I don't know who or what I want.
> *Frankie (14)*

> I think about this guy all the time. He's really handsome and makes me laugh, but I couldn't tell anyone how I felt because they'd beat me up. A guy at school said he was gay and he got bullied every day after that. Anyway, I don't know if I am gay or not because sometimes I fancy girls. It's hard having to be so secretive. I mean, how am I ever going to find out what I want if I can't talk to anyone about it?
> *Jules (16)*

The fact is, although the majority of the population turn out to be heterosexual, a high proportion of straight people have some sort of gay experience in their life, usually around adolescent time. However, whatever you think, do, and feel doesn't mean you're suddenly one thing or another. Our sexuality is not fixed upon one emotional and/or sexual experience or fantasy. It's something that grows and matures with the rest of our body, personality, and mind. So, to be sexually stirred by someone of your own sex is no indication of what your sexual orientation is or will be. Likewise, nor is having a crush, fantasy, or feelings of love towards someone of your own sex.

> I was in the showers after a football match at my local club when I became aware of this guy's body. I couldn't help looking at it and suddenly became turned on. I was so disgusted at myself. I couldn't believe what I was doing. I kept thinking 'What if he'd seen me?' 'What am I doing?' I was so upset that I gave up football (which I love) because I couldn't bear to face him again.
> *Stuart (16)*

It is important to realize that during adolescence a boy's body starts to develop its basis for sexual arousal. At this stage it isn't very choosy about what it responds to, and anything could cause you to become sexually aroused. This is why most boys end up having to hide erections on buses, in showers, or even when a person brushes too close to them. All it is is an automatic response to intimacy and nothing to worry about at all, because it will soon learn to control itself and become more selective.

Homophobia and homosexual fantasies

Homophobia is the root of why the majority of boys with crushes on someone of their own sex stay silent and become miserable. Homophobia is an irrational hatred of homosexuals, and, if you don't think this is true, just take a look around you. Gay people are still penalized for being honest about their feelings, they are beaten up for just walking down the street together, and words like 'poof', 'queer', and 'dyke' are used so frequently they've almost become part of the English language.

The basis for this kind of ignorant behaviour in people is fear. Fear of the unknown, fear of their own confused sexual feelings, and fear, in the words of one 13-year-old boy, that 'it might be catching'. Not only is this behaviour anti-social but in all cases it is against everything our culture supposedly stands for.

> There's a guy at our school who is openly gay and I used to hate him and pick on him till one day he turned on me and asked me what I was afraid of. He asked if I fancied some guy or something. I was speechless and tried to say something but I ended up looking like a fool, because he'd sussed me completely.
> *Tony (15)*

Sexuality is a fundamental part of who we are, and if we have to hide our feelings and deny who we are it can cause a huge amount of pain and suffering. Learning to be honest about how and what you feel is an important part of learning how to be a worthwhile human being. This doesn't mean that you have to rush to label yourself, because, as we've already seen, thinking you are in love with someone of the same sex doesn't necessarily mean you're gay, straight, or bisexual.

In fact, I was at school with a girl who had a boyfriend constantly from the time she was fourteen years old. She was the one person who made the rest of us feel insecure about the lack of boyfriends and attention we received because she always had armies of guys after her. Recently, I bumped into her and was surprised to find she had been having an affair with a woman for four years. She said she had never realized she felt this way until she went away to college. The moral of this story is, whatever happens during your teenage years is no sure indication of how you're going to feel in the future.

CRUSHES ON BOYS

If this is the case, then don't declare how you feel about someone to everyone and anyone. Apart from the fact it is an invitation to disaster, it will mean a free-for-all when it comes to intrusion into your private life. After all, what you feel, choose to do, and who you love is up to you and you alone. It's private, it's personal, and not something that needs to be debated by every Nosy Parker in the world.

> I confided in my best friend that I was quite turned on by this male model's body. The next think I knew, my friends were all keeping clear of me, and my mum was crying and asking if it was true I was gay. The fact is I only dream about this guy and that's all. I also fancy girls, but I am so fed up with everyone trying to find out what I am, when I don't even know.
> *Duncan (15)*

As you can see from the rest of this book, experiencing a crush and having something real are two different things entirely. The fantasies we have when we have a crush on someone are daydreams and their biggest pleasure is often that they won't happen in the real world.

> Yes, I dream about my friends sometimes. I imagine being with them and stuff like that, but I'd die if one of them turned round to me and said 'come on then'. I don't want it to come real. It's just nice to imagine what it would be like. I'm just curious.
> *Nick (17)*

It's not easy to know what you are. Some people swear they are sure from a very young age, while others in their late 30s are still trying to figure it out. If your crushes are confusing, don't rush to squash all your feelings. Apart from being near impossible to do effectively, it's far healthier to go with them. Let your emotions see-saw until they find the side or balance they want.

I try not to let my crush on Gary make me so unhappy. He knows how I feel because it's so obvious and he's told me straight that he doesn't feel the same. That was hard to take but at least he is still my best friend and I know where I stand.
David (17)

I was so unhappy and lonely at boarding school until I fell in love. I had really strong feelings for an older boy. He was in my thoughts all the time for three years and on two occasions we even kissed. I convinced myself that this was true love for me, but when I left school and started working I fell in love with this girl and started dating her. I felt for her all the same things I had felt for this guy. Now I can see that my feelings for him weren't an indication that I was gay but an indication that I was desperate for some love and affection, and I am still grateful for that.
Hamish (23)

Common crushes

If you've got a crush, it's easy to think you're the only one who feels this way. After all, no one ever voices their feelings too openly about love, especially when it's love of someone of the same sex. But don't be afraid. You're just experiencing something completely normal, and you're not alone. If you knew how many people agonized over their sexuality and feelings you'd be surprised.

The most common crush that boys experience occurs on older boys. This is because an older man is usually the most available role model around. It is easy to become fixated on someone who is older and more experienced than you, and it's just as easy for this admiration to turn into something much deeper.

I was really into motorbikes and would hang out at the tracks every weekend. There was this guy, he was really popular with the other guys, he had lovely women round him and won a lot

CRUSHES ON BOYS

of the races. He started talking to me one day and I was really flattered. The next think I knew I had started fantasizing about him and imagining that we were really close. It was a real shock to me.
Tim (17)

The fact is many of us have crushes on our role models, mainly because we want more than to be close to them. We want to be them.

Role models as crushes are an important way of finding out the kind of person you want to be. Most people with same-sex crushes on people they admire eventually become that kind of person, and this in later years finally gives them an answer for why they felt so passionate about someone of their own sex.

Loneliness at school is another reason why some boys end up having a crush on another boy. The fact is, if you are at an all-boys school, you're not likely to meet many girls whom you can develop a crush on. And we already know that a crush is a healthy outlet for all that frustration and anxiety over love. Therefore, if you don't have any girls around, or don't know any girls to talk to, then a boy is your only alternative.

I just don't know how to talk to girls. I don't understand them. They confuse me terribly and because of this I don't fancy them. Instead I find myself attracted to boys, which does worry me. You see, I live with my Dad and brothers, and none of them are dating, so we tend to just mix with other guys.
Steve (15)

I am always fancying boys in my school, because they are on the same wavelength as me. The girls I know are so drippy. They like to see soppy films, go shopping, and gossip with their friends. They just aren't interested in the same things as me, so how can I even start to fancy them?
Jim (14)

CRUSHES ON BOYS

Lots of boys at my boarding school had affairs with other boys and we all had crushes on each other. But it wasn't some kind of debauched school, it was the only way we could deal with puberty. There were no girls around and we weren't allowed into the village to talk to them. Now, five years later, all of us are either dating girls madly or getting married. So you see, those days were quite harmless for us all.
Jake (23)

What to do if your crush is getting you down

So now you know it's perfectly natural to feel something for someone of your own sex, just how do you deal with those feelings of misery and unrequited love?

1 Don't feel guilty about it.

Guilt is the biggest guarantee of unhappiness and misery. It makes us feel like we've done something wrong and that we deserve to be punished. Having a crush is about none of these things. It's about experiencing love without having to go through its ups and downs. This means it's guilt free because you haven't actually done anything. Think of it this way: imagine someone you know upsets you badly. You wish them dead but don't actually do anything. Do you deserve to be tried and found guilty for a crime you haven't even committed? No, of course you don't. The same thing applies to crushes. There's nothing wrong with loving someone of the same sex and nothing wrong with having a crush on them. So, don't beat yourself up with feelings of guilt and remorse. Just take your feelings for what they are – affection for someone you admire.

2 Talk about your feelings.

This is an important part of learning to deal with your crush. If you keep all your feelings bottled up inside you, they'll just grow and grow until they explode. Of course, you have to pick the person you tell very carefully, unless you want your feelings to become common knowledge. If you have an understanding parent or older sibling, they would be your best bet as friends have a knack of letting things slip. Some people find talking to someone they don't know the best help. There are a variety of helplines that are completely confidential and will talk to anyone concerned about their sexual identity (numbers at end of the book) – The Albany Trust, Lesbian and Gay Switchboard, London Friend.

3 Don't rush to any conclusions.

This is the route of most unhappiness when it comes to same-sex crushes. Jumping from the beginning of an equation to the end without experiencing the middle is dangerous. Feeling love for another boy isn't, as we've already said, a sure sign you are gay. Likewise, feeling unhappy about love and the things that come with it isn't a sign that this is what love is like. Real love isn't just in your mind and, because it's more tangible, it's easier to deal with the down parts.

4 Experimenting is just experimenting.

There's a popular saying that goes 'You have to kiss an awful lot of frogs before you find your Prince Charming'. The same goes for crushes. You have to feel most things before you can decide what's right and what's wrong for you. It doesn't mean that you'll fall in love with everyone and everything before you find true love, but it does mean that you'll experience feelings of love for a diverse lot of people before you find your match. It's a bit like shopping for a perfect pair of jeans. What you thought fitted you perfectly when you were fifteen years old, isn't likely to be perfect for you when you're twenty-five years old.

> It's only when I look back now that I can see that every crush and relationship I had, whether it was on someone male, female, or famous, helped me to come a step closer to what I

wanted. Now I am happily married to a girl who I'm madly and passionately in love with.
Hamish (23)

5 Enjoy your crush.

This is the most important part of crushes. They may be there to learn about love from, they may be there to feel what it's like when someone doesn't love you back, but they are there especially to be enjoyed. Everything that happens is at your control, you can make them happy or sad, you can make the person be nice to you or nasty. Whatever happens, it's all part of the enjoyment of being in love in your mind. If you refuse to let other people make you feel stupid, guilty, or weak about them, and don't let them take over your life, they can be a wonderful experience and one that you'll remember for the rest of your life.

Useful Addresses

- **Careline**
Tel. 081 514 1177
A helpline for any teenager worried and/or distressed about a problem.

- **Childline**
Tel. 0800 1111
24-hour confidential advice service for young people.

- **Relate** (National Marriage Guidance Council)
Little Church Street
Rugby CV21 3AP
If you have a relationship problem and can't find a youth counsellor near you, then RELATE may be able to help.

- **Samaritans**
Details in your local directory under 'S', or call the operator on 100 and ask to be connected.

- **Youth Access**
Magazine Business Centre
11 Newarke Street
Leicester LE1 5SS
A referral agency for youth counselling services. Send s.a.e. for details.

If you need someone to talk to about your sexual identity, contact any of the following. They are all sympathetic and completely confidential.

USEFUL ADDRESSES

- **The Albany Trust**
Sunra Centre
26 Balham Hill
London SW12 9EB
Tel. 081 675 6669

- **Lesbian and Gay Switchboard**
BM Switchboard
London WC1N 3XX
Tel. 071 837 7324 – a 24-hour helpline for people worried about their sexuality.

- **London Friend**
86 Caledonian Road
London N1 9DN
Tel. 071 837 3337